BRACE FOR IMPACT

Re-Thinking Safety in Today's America

Michael Marks

i

ISBN   978-0-9861521-1-5

For my mom,
who showed me that beauty and toughness went hand in hand,
who raised me to be a knight in shining armor,
and who never backed down from a fight.

ACKNOWLEDGEMENTS

This book is a compilation of knowledge graciously provided by numerous law enforcement officers and trainers, school teachers, administrators and paramedics as well as members of the U.S. Special Operations training cadre both home and abroad. Many of these are the people who run in when everyone else is running away. You all rock.

I must once again acknowledge Ted Deeds for a an absolute wealth of subject matter expertise on police, emergency response and legal considerations. Another important thank you goes to Edgar "Big Al" Sibert and all the terrific men and women at Virginia's Frederick County Sheriff's Department. A continual stream of thanks goes Barry Solomon for his peerless review and analysis, and for following me into any project, big or small. Thanks also to my superb models, Elizabeth Carty and Griffin Fox.

And as always, to my wife, for her constant support and encouragement.

TABLE OF CONTENTS

FORWARD

Over the last two generations, our nation has experienced a profound and disturbing change. Society is increasingly uncivil, intolerant and violent on a scale that few could have imagined just a generation ago. Today we see crime in our streets and homes; horrific attacks on our schools, theaters, shops, and on places of work and worship. Although these atrocities have been sadly commonplace on foreign soil, it is a different matter for us when it happens here.

In the wake of these events, the arms of our government flail in opposing directions. Some legislators work to keep criminals behind bars while others push parole and early release. We've seen guns banned in some areas while gun ownership has become mandatory in others. We've seen some schools train their own teachers how to shoot while other schools file criminal charges against small children over half-eaten pastry some teacher deemed to resemble a gun. Police departments tell citizens to arm themselves while anti-gun groups say we should be disarmed. There is no national logic, no unified vision. In this storm of conflicting direction, who knows what to do?

Other social forces further complicate the problem. While nations like Cyprus and Greece slide violently into financial ruin, Americans see major U.S. cities as large as Detroit declare bankruptcy. At this time, nearly two dozen cities in California alone are officially in severe financial crisis. Our once-robust economy has faltered and millions of Americans are out of work.

As a spin-off of this situation, our public discourse is increasingly injected with the poison of class warfare which cries that the "haves" are to blame for the woes of the "have nots." Families and business owners who were once looked upon as having earned the benefits of hard work and sacrifice are now vilified as among the "one percent" whose greed has left the rest to suffer. With unsettling frequency that debate has hinted that the time has come for those without to take what they deserve, by force if necessary.

These disturbing trends become even more troubling if you understand the limits of our law enforcement and emergency response capacity. Most of us hold to the comforting myth that police will magically appear to save us in our time of need. Sadly, the majority of police departments across the country lack the manpower to do so and by law have no obligation to try. Understaffed 911 systems have openly stated that they cannot manage the volume of incoming calls. Average response times to a true emergency run longer than the average duration of a violent attack. If something really bad happens, this response gap can and does stretch to the breaking point. In the aftermath of Hurricane Sandy, entire neighborhoods were left to face the approaching dead of a brutal winter without power, phone or emergency services for months on end. During that time, home-wrecked citizens were on their own to fend off looters as well as the elements.

This reality begs the obvious question: where does the average American turn for guidance? While volumes have been written on the subject of personal and family defense, many of them are as thick as a phone book and read like a FEMA training manual. They are steeped in academic theory or military jargon when all we really want to know is how to get out of trouble... or better yet how to avoid trouble altogether.

In writing *Brace For Impact*, author Michael Marks has distilled a lifetime of police and special operations training experience into a concise, plain-English resource for the average citizen that is both eye-opening and thought-provoking. He explains the realities of today's violent crime with clear analogies that anyone can understand. He presents observations that are not watered down with political correctness, nor burdened with academic pride. Although *Brace For Impact* does not try to paint a gloomy picture, it also does not offer a sugar-coated view that things will magically work out. Some of the observations in this book may be called cynical, but that cynicism is widely shared by people on both ends of the political spectrum.

From the onset, *Brace For Impact* is focused on the vital questions of *what*; what happens to people every day and what can we do to avoid, escape or defeat those hazards. The courses of action presented here do not ask the reader to channel their inner Jason Bourne, in fact quite the opposite is true. This book is written for the average man or woman, mom or dad, son or daughter. Mr. Marks lays out a range of simple steps you can adopt to fit your lifestyle, your age and your physical abilities. *Brace For Impact* provides a wealth of tools to help the average American make sense out of concerns we all share and to make what are often minor adjustments that can greatly improve your safety, awareness and state of mind.

Carl Rowan Jr.
Former FBI Special Agent
and Deputy U.S. Marshal

x

A Matter of Perspective

Bobby and Jessica went camping in the rugged mountains of Montana. After a long day of hiking they found themselves in front of a crackling campfire. The night air was heavy with the delicious smell of burning wood and hot dogs.

The quiet was broken by the snap of a branch somewhere in the darkness. Bobby peered out and saw a pair of amber eyes glowing in the firelight. Then a second pair. Then a third. Something growled.

"Oh my God," Bobby gasped. "Wolves."

Jessica looked around, nodded silently in agreement, then began to rummage in her backpack.

The golden eyes moved closer, the fog of feral breath now ghostly white amid the trees. Panic crawled up Bobby's spine. "If you've got a gun in there," he stammered, "you better hurry."

With a grunt of satisfaction Jessica pulled out a pair of bright-colored Nike track shoes. Bobby felt his jaw fall open in surprise; he had always thought of Jess as a clear-thinking girl.

"Are you out of your mind?" he hissed, "You can't outrun a pack of wolves!"

Cinching down the laces Jessica stood, smiled and gave him a gentle pat on the shoulder and said

**"I don't have to outrun the wolves silly,
I just have to outrun you."**

INTRODUCTION

"Those who do not learn from history are doomed to repeat it."
~ George Santayana

The opening story about wolves may seem like a bit of dark humor, but a cold reality runs deep in the punch line. At a most basic level the Earth is one big interconnected food chain, a revolving dance of predators and prey. Many things on this planet live by killing and eating other creatures. In that race, the prize for being the slowest is a center seat on the dinner plate.

For the most part, survival in nature does not hinge on fighting off an attacker. Fighting is risky business and everybody in a fight tends to get hurt to some degree. Instead, creatures great and small have developed very effective strategies to avoid being the one that catches the predator's eye in the first place. From herds to schools to flocks, animals around the world have developed survival behaviors that rely on somebody else being just a step slower, somebody else looking just a bit tastier.

It sounds ugly but predation is as much a part of human nature as a wolf's penchant for hunting. Just like you, criminals have to eat and pay bills, but unlike moral people they choose to take what they need by force. Some criminals possess a hunger for violence, others might be drugged up or outright insane. You may not like these notions, but the truth -- as seen in our daily headlines -- is utterly undeniable. Human violence takes a bloody bite out of millions upon millions of people every year; it has for all of history and it will for as long as man exists.

If you are like a lot of people, you recognize that violence is a genuine problem but you tell yourself it will happen to somebody else. Denial is a common way of coping with all sorts of threats, but denial doesn't do you much good when the problem stares you in the face. In fact, ignoring a hazard usually makes things worse. Denial is just gambling, doing nothing because you don't know what to do and hoping that you get lucky.

Mind you, some people do get lucky, like those who drive drunk time and time again and make it home unscathed. Some boast that their survival in the face of repeated irresponsibility disproves the threat altogether, right up to the point when their bodies are found wrapped around a telephone pole.

You are free to gamble that the violence around us all will always happen to somebody else, but if you do, keep one thing in mind; **your neighborhood and workplace are filled with people who are betting it will happen to you.** Somebody in that group is going to be right.

1

Any competent gambler will tell you that before you place a bet, you ought to know how much you are willing to risk versus what you stand to win, and the odds of either outcome. The risks from violent crime vary widely, from minor injury to trauma that would make for a horror movie. Examples fill our recent headlines. Some lunatic shoots up a kindergarten, another blows up a building. A child is molested by a teacher or priest while other kids are imprisoned in a neighbor's house and subjected to years of rape and torture. One bully in school drives a girl to suicide while a different bully is stabbed to death by a group of victims who couldn't take any more. Even unthinkable terms like cannibal attack and public beheading now have modern-day relevance.

These events -- and things far, far worse -- happen to somebody every day, a person who consciously or otherwise had bet his or her life on the belief that it would happen to somebody else.

That's a bummer, I know, but as depressing as it may sound, the statistical odds against the average citizen will not get better with time, in fact they are going to get worse. That is not alarmist rhetoric, but mathematical certainty. Consider the factors:

While we grapple with our fears, legislators on both sides of the political fence are too wrapped up selling ideology and making deals to have an open, honest debate about anything. We are polarized to the point of national paralysis. Look for yourself: after almost fifteen years to improve how we deal with school shootings, the kids at Sandy Hill Elementary in 2012 fared no better than those at Columbine in 1999. The victims of Hurricane Sandy in 2012 suffered as badly as those in the wake of Katrina in 1995.

Oh, to be certain we are spending money on our problems, tons of money in fact, but we are not making things any better. The act of simply spending money is not a solution. As citizens we watch silently as one administration after another throws billions upon trillions of taxpayer dollars into a giant Black Hole of undefined ideas that carry no metrics for success. In 2014 the GSA (the book-keepers of the Federal Government) announced that some $619 Billion was "just gone" and nobody could account for it. Our legislators have become so arrogant that they publicly admit to passing bills they haven't even read. Government ineptitude has reached the point that after spending untold billions of dollars, it could even launch a website. It is no wonder that things in our society only get worse.

The mainstream media is no help, for reasons far more fundamental than the conspiratorial assertions that they are all aligned in some sort of world-shaping, evil, cabal. The simple truth is that the news industry is a business for profit that runs on advertising revenues, which in turn are based on the number of viewers. A sizeable portion of our TV-watching audience lost interest in the truth, or frankly in any story that requires thinking. We have increasingly become a world of reality TV, public temper tantrums and crass, tawdry behavior.

News programs serving that audience have no incentive to waste effort in the search for facts. Research is time-consuming and expensive. Their business is more profitable dishing out divisive "info-tainment" that is only loosely based on current events. They compete for brief attention spans with sensationalism, scandal and political anger. Society at large has issued no widespread demand for coverage of dull issues like fiscal accountability or Constitutional rights. They choose instead to fill their day with every moment of insipid behavior acted out on the public stage by the ilk of Justin Bieber or Lindsay Lohan.

As a result, much of what has become known as the mainstream media feeds us spin and slogans in lieu of facts, making up details to fill in the gaps before moving on to the next lurid, divisive or outright fictitious story. With rare exceptions, the time-honored notions of class, dignity and journalistic integrity embodied in names like Edward R. Murrow or Walter Cronkite are all but extinct.

Society itself is too divided, distracted or simply too discouraged to try and hold even our own elected officials accountable, no matter how bad the crime. Nobody has any sense of what a trillion dollars is, or what it means when we are $17 trrillion in debt as a nation. The numbers are too big to understand. Our problems have become so overwhelming they blur together into a haze of worry, fear and helplessness. Absent any leadership on the issue of criminal violence, people are left to ask "why?"

Why do bad people do such brutal things?

Why can't governments find a common-sense solution?

A thousand books have raised those weighty questions and have beaten a thousand dead horses into the ground. This isn't one of those books, and for good reason. **Despite all of our intellectual curiosity, "why" doesn't matter. Not to you, not to your family.** The why will be violently debated for the next hundred years and at the end of all that time, no two experts will agree. We are not a month or a year or a decade away from understanding what makes people do sick, crazy things. We will not have an answer before your child graduates high school or college, or before their children do in turn. If you peel away the self-confidence inherent in science you will find the simple fact that despite all we have learned about the human mind, we really haven't got a clue as to what makes people tick.

Now admittedly, the Big Picture of human behavior is important to mankind on some grand level and good luck to all those who work to unravel the mysteries of the brain, but the rest of us have to live our lives in the meantime. Our families have to avoid the road ragers, the child molesters, the drug dealers, kidnappers, bullies and rapists who can make life on this earth a horrible experience. We have to face these challenges without Secret Service agents, hired bodyguards or armored cars. We have to do it every single day, on a family budget, in between work, soccer practice and grocery shopping. To do this, we have to quit asking "why" and start asking "what."

"What happens if...?"

Think of it this way: very few Americans can explain in any scientific detail why a whole bunch of electricity can kill us. It is a physics and anatomy question that involves words like *fibrillation* and *conductivity*. It is a "why" question that for most of us doesn't matter. What DOES matter is knowing what happens if you stick a butter knife in a wall socket. **Zap - you're dead**. That is a clear nugget of knowledge you can easily understand and use to make some smart decisions. Little kids can grasp that message long before they understand the why of voltage and amperes. That little nugget of "what" saves lives every day.

This book is written to give you an equally clear understanding of the three most fundamental "what" questions that should define your plans and expectations for safety:

What can happen if I find myself in a bad event?

What can I do to avoid being there in the first place?

What can I do to get out?

Having spent a lifetime training military, law enforcement and emergency response personnel in places ranging from the USA to Afghanistan, I have chosen to address those questions in blunt, common-sense terms. This book is not written like so many others to instill some pointless fear that the boogeyman is under the bed, nor is it some sort of "OMG - PANIC" guide to surviving the Zombie Apocalypse. Yes, violent crime is a problem, in some places a bad problem, so let's deal with it intelligently.

Fear is disabling, knowledge is empowering.
Fear consumes your time, knowledge frees you to enjoy your time.

Brace For Impact is about realistic little steps, many of them free and utterly invisible to others, that can give you peace of mind in your day-to-day life and a big head start if things start to go bad. It is unabashedly straight about the reality of the joke that opened this book. Criminals, like wolves, look for the weak, the slow and the clueless. You do not have to become Chuck Norris nor should you likely choose to fight criminals head-on as a first preference. In many cases you just need to appear a little better prepared or a little more aware than the most oblivious people around you, and trust me, they are in abundance. The criminal's own target selection process will often take care of the rest. That may seem harsh but in any predator -versus-herd scenario somebody has to take one for the team; you just need to make sure you don't end up with that honor.

Throughout this book I am very up-front about my beliefs. I will not try to sell you a hidden agenda buried in subtext. The politics of personal safety, of defending yourself or the potential role of a gun in that effort, continue to derail candid public discussion.

As such, I have chosen to open my presentation with a very blunt chapter on the politics of self-defense to get past the rhetoric. I do not believe that everybody should have a gun nor do I care if you have one or not. Either decision will carry both strengths and liabilities. *Brace For Impact* will discuss these so you can make an informed, intelligent decision.

As a matter of practice in all matters of importance, and especially ones regarding your safety, I urge you to question any assertion given to you. Even so-called experts or national figures can offer some extremely dumb advice. In 2013 Vice President Joe Biden appeared on national television telling American women that the proper response to a frightening sound outside the house was to fire two shotgun blasts into the air. This will be discussed in more detail in Section Two but suffice for the moment to say that this is a catastrophically stupid notion that can result in injury, litigation and criminal prosecution. Sadly, that didn't stop the news media who carried it as sound advice from our Vice President. People following this advice (and there are documented cases) discovered that discharging a firearm as some sort of warning is a crime in many locations.

The sad truth is that we live in a world where ignorant, uninformed and out-of-context sound bites are presented as gospel and repeated endlessly across the media and internet. Celebrities and politicians are among the most notorious for making outrageous statements without the support of subject matter knowledge or simple science.

You should never accept any statement regarding your safety, no matter what the source,
without checking the facts for yourself.

ORGANIZATION

For your convenience, this book is organized into two sections.

Section One is written for people who are unfamiliar with the notions of crime, violence and self-defense. It does so by building upward from the most fundamental levels. It will establish a foundation of facts and logic that can support intelligent analysis. As mentioned above, it addresses, in order, the questions important to our day-to-day safety:

What can hurt me?	(Threat)
What are the odds of this happening?	(Probability)
What is the worst possible outcome?	(Severity)
What can I count on to save me?	(Mitigation)

There are no surprise answers; most of the real wisdom in life is based on common sense. You may however be shocked to learn just how frequently violent crime occurs, how bad it can be, or that nobody may be standing by to save us in our moment of need.

In reality, the four pillars of Threat, Probability, Severity and Mitigation are the cornerstones of a 4.3 trillion dollar insurance industry as well as countless Threat and Vulnerability Assessments performed by military and intelligence personnel every day. This is how professionals break down a problem set in order to define avoidance strategies and countermeasures. While that might sound like some great action-movie lingo, it simply means that professionals insist on having a plan to stay safe and so should you. At the end of Section One you should have a solid, real-world understanding of your risks, the impact on your life, and the resources upon which you can rely when the chips are down.

Section Two is a set of practical tools focused on taking care of yourself at the individual, family, workplace and community levels. It is in part scenario-based, presenting some widely seen situations and examining a range of possible responses and outcomes. Tossing some more lingo at you, these techniques, tactics and procedures (TTPs) prioritize awareness and avoidance over more overt defense alternatives. Section Two will refer to resources that can be downloaded from the *Brace For Impact* website. These can serve as the backbone of a sound Family Security Plan, be it a family at home or at a workplace or school.

If you have already found yourself at the wrong end of a violent or threatening scenario, you likely have a far more vivid appreciation for the dynamics involved. Faced with a dangerous opponent, seconds can feel like an eternity and mere yards to safety can feel like miles. No matter how desperately we need somebody at that moment, help does not parachute out of the sky or appear in a Harry Potter-esque puff of smoke.

To make matters worse, it has become increasingly rare in modern society to see an eyewitness lift a finger to help someone in need. While we thankfully still have heroes in our midst, detached spectators are often more interested in catching video to post on YouTube than they are in calling 911 or rendering aid. It is not realistic to expect people around you to come to your assistance, even when they would be at no risk to do so.

Case Study: Glenwood Gardens
A chilling example of inhuman detachment took place in February of 2013 when a nurse at the Glenwood Gardens nursing home in Bakersfield, California blatantly refused 911 instructions to provide CPR to 87-year-old Lorraine Bayless who lay dying. In the nationally publicized recording of the phone conversation, the nurse advised 911 that providing CPR to save a life was "not company policy." Despite frantic pleas by the 911 operator to help, or to find anybody who would help, the nurse did nothing and watched the woman die.

The scenario above is not consistent with the America in which many of us grew up, and I would presume it was not likely the America Ms. Bayless expected to be in when her life was on the line. **The belief -- or perhaps the desperate hope -- that a brave and capable fellow citizen will help us is no longer a certainty.**

This is not purely coincidence; to a measurable degree our own court system promotes this type of heartlessness. We have a judicial system that is all too willing to punish a selfless act of heroism with equal if not greater emphasis than the criminal who started the problem in the first place. In this book you will see how intervening on behalf of somebody else, no matter how noble the sentiment or just the cause, may carry consequences for you that extend far beyond the immediate incident and injury. Not all hazards stem from a dangerous felon.

As you read this book I challenge you, in the quiet privacy of your own heart, to push aside the veneer of social etiquette or fashionable politics that define our world. Ask yourself if the cherished notions of a Norman Rockwell America, as heart-warming as they may be, match the world you see around you. Then take steps to be safe in the world you actually live in, instead of the world we all wish we had.

THE POLITICS OF PERSONAL SAFETY

"Praemonitus praemunitus" ~ forewarned is forearmed

As put forth in the Introduction, this book has no interest in advancing the agenda of any political party. Nothing written here will affect the legislative direction of our nation. But politicians and bureaucrats have a huge impact on our lives and we should recognize the power of politics to shape the world in which we live.

If there is one thing that most Americans across the political landscape can agree on, it is that no matter which way the political pendulum swings, our government is a train wreck. As this is being written, the approval rating for Congress hovers around a dismal 12%. From one administration to the next the gross mismanagement of our collective leaders has been driving families, businesses, cities and entire states into bankruptcy. Legislators openly admit to passing laws without reading them and they refuse to stop spending our money long after the money has run out. Our elected officials commit crimes of immense scale and blatantly refuse to answer to the very public that pays their salaries.

> I submit this not as a rant or gripe, but merely to support a heartfelt assertion:
> **These are not the people you should trust with your safety.**

That said, any realistic discussion of self-defense must at some point touch on the subject of guns. They are a reality for good and for bad, just like everything else. In our society, any mention of a gun will immediately be cast as taking a political stand. Groups on both sides of the gun debate will scream that if you are not 100% in their camp, you are 100% in the other. The tone has become shrill and venomous, increasingly laced with name-calling and threats of violence. It is pretty obvious why we have no meaningful discussion on the subject.

Thus, in the interest of being transparent from the start, I have collected the basis for what will doubtlessly be cast as my politically-oriented statements into this one chapter. These points are presented not to promote or vilify guns but merely to dispel misconceptions that prevent us from making clear, accurate decisions based on fact.

The analysis you will find in this book is based on three fundamental beliefs which may seem, on their face, to have nothing to do with safety or criminal violence. They would, however, have an immense impact on how we deal with criminal violence if applied to national-level policy and will have direct impact on your well-being if you apply them to your safety planning. These fundamentals are:

Think First, Spend Later

Whether as individuals or collectively as a nation, we should not spend a dollar of taxpayer money until we know what we can expect in return. I am not talking some wild guess or shiny promise but a sound, supportable justification. I can explain to you with solid science what benefit you get from having a seatbelt in your car; I cannot rationally predict what benefit you would get, if any, from slapping a "Crash-Free Zone" sign on your front bumper. Diligence prior to spending outweighs anything done afterwards.

Check for Success

If we do not get what we paid for, we need to find out why and revise our spending decisions. Tax-spenders should be accountable to tax-payers. No matter how pretty or poetic it might sound, a bad idea is a bad idea and you don't make a failed program work by spending more money on it. But we do just that for failed safety ideas year in and year out and citizens pay the price with their lives.

Waste Nothing

As families, or all together as a nation, we do not have a bottomless pit of cash and we don't have forever. If we waste time and money on a foolish errand today, we are literally burning resources that might otherwise have supported an effective solution. There is an axiom among soldiers: "You cannot miss fast enough to win a gunfight." When a tragic event happens in America, legislators scramble to fire taxpayer dollars without aiming. We must demand answers that can provide demonstrable results in keeping us safe today... or we ought to demand smarter legislators.

With those fundamentals as a basis, this book holds as true the following common-sense series of assertions:

1) **If you are being attacked, you want the strongest weapon available**; ideally a better weapon than the one being used against you. If you are not Chuck Norris, a baseball bat is probably stronger than empty hands. A knife makes a better weapon than a spoon and a German Shepherd will likely protect you more than a Chihuahua. The reason the Army has the Abrams tank is because nobody has invented something bigger and deadlier. If you are in danger, you want the most effective tool available.

2) **For its size, a gun is the most powerful combative tool man has invented**. That is why we give guns to our soldiers and police officers. No other device can do more to cancel out the disparities of age, gender, strength or speed. If Tasers or pepper spray were as effective as guns, our soldiers would carry them into battle. Anyone who tells you otherwise is lying or insipid. Every city and town in America relies on armed officers to protect places like banks, hospitals, airports and schools because an armed individual works better than anything else we have today to deter or interrupt violent crime. Even the politicians who tell you otherwise protect themselves with guns.

3) **A gun is a piece of metal, devoid of life or magical powers**. Evil spirits do not rise from a gun if you melt it. A gun cannot force someone to shoot it any more than a car can force someone to drive. Violence is a human choice, driven by human factors like greed, immaturity, emotion, insanity or sheer malevolence. If guns had never been invented mankind as a species would still be killing each other just as energetically; we would just be using things like knives, hammers and rocks.

4) **The value of any tool, from a lowly screwdriver to an expensive car, depends on knowing how to use it.** Realistic training should be a critical component of everything you do with respect to your safety and the safety of others. That applies to guns, Tasers, pepper sprays, house alarms and anything else upon which you will rely for your protection. A wise coach once told me "There's no replacement for knowing what you are doing."

5) **A gun is not the right answer for everybody, nor should everybody have access to a gun.** Our society is filled with people who demonstrate various combinations of genuine evil, malignant irresponsibility and blinding stupidity. In a logical world these people should not be allowed to have guns, or cars for that matter. Some should be kept away from sharp objects. Even a rock, in the hands of an idiot, is a disaster waiting to happen. Sadly we do not live in a logical world and keeping dangerous objects out of the hands of irresponsible people is a problem that society will never, ever solve.

6) **The number of guns in the world is approaching one billion** and an estimated 310 million of them are in the United States. Millions more are manufactured every year. In impoverished third-world nations, modern-style guns are built by hand every day with tools that would be considered primitive by American standards. Using no more than hobby-level CNC tools and 3D printers, very high quality guns can be manufactured in garage workshops. Beyond that, our porous borders allow millions of people to enter this country with no inspection, so we have no idea how many guns come in with them. No matter what bans our government decides to issue, guns will no more disappear from city streets than illicit drugs or alcohol did when they were banned. Whether or not guns are outlawed, whether or not you choose to have a gun, you can be certain that lots of other people -- both good and bad -- will have them.

7) **Our criminal justice system fails to keep even the most violent of criminals off the streets.** Murderers, rapists and child molesters view the prison system little more than a temporary inconvenience. Roughly 80% of the inmates in maximum security prison end up released back into the public where a significant majority of them commit subsequent crimes. Looking at actual examples, it is clear that our penal system is incapable of keeping even the most vicious animals locked away from the rest of us.

No matter how brutally realistic these might seem, these seven points will confound and enrage a great many people because they trample back and forth over traditional "gun control vs. gun rights" dogmas. They are not offered in support of a liberal or conservative agenda, but rather as common sense, something that is all too absent in public discourse. You can choose to dismiss any of these points if you like but you would be hard-pressed to refute them in the face of the supporting evidence.

It is often overlooked in the course of public debate that an armed citizen has no obligation to use any weapon in his possession. An armed citizen is as free as anybody else to run, hide, scream for help or pursue any other form of defensive action. The difference between an armed and unarmed citizen is that when both have exhausted all possible options for escape or rescue, the armed citizen is better equipped to forestall injury through the use of force. In the case of a firearm in competent hands, that option can have a considerable impact on the outcome of a fight.

So what does this mean to you? Well, you can certainly choose to live without a gun, millions of people do, but one day you may face somebody who has one, or who is a whole lot bigger and stronger than you are. Conversely, you can buy a gun for protection but one day find yourself without it in a moment of need. An unsecured gun in your home or vehicle may fall into untrained or irresponsible hands and cause terrible harm. You may in the worst of cases actually use a gun in self-defense only to find yourself buried beneath an unexpected mountain of legal or emotional trouble afterwards.

Simply put, there are no risk-free answers: any choice you make will come with its own hazards. No matter what your politics, you would be well-served to understand both sides of the gun issue and have a solid plan to keep your family safe no matter what happens. In times of crisis, surprises are usually bad.

Whatever you decide, whatever you choose to rely upon in a crunch, don't kid yourself. If you are lucky the price for an unsafe decision or unrealistic expectation might be no more than an embarrassing moment, but for some people it has been life-changing injury or death. If you do not consciously choose to learn about things that present a danger to you, you are just as actively choosing to be ignorant of them.

> **Ignorance is not stupidity, ignorance is merely being uninformed on a subject. Choosing ignorance is stupidity.**

Always remember, a lack of education assures that any decision you make, especially under the stress of physical danger, will be the least-informed and least-likely to result in a safe outcome.

POLITICS VERSUS EDUCATION

If politics are rampant in the debate on guns, do they touch on our safety education process as well? Sadly, the answer is a resounding yes.

Honest education can provide citizens and legislators with clear, accurate information upon which to base a smart, fact-based decision. Consider for just a moment how we deal with our kids. When politics are not in play, we give our children very frank lessons about any hazards they might face in life. Our schools have classes in sex education, driver safety, drug education, classes on smoking and alcohol, courses on avoiding bullies and sexual predators. These are awful, ugly topics. Yet we teach our kids about them knowing that one day our children may face a tough choice with grave repercussions and we want them to be armed with the best knowledge to make the smartest, safest decision.

If we hold that education is a safeguard against every other conceivable threat, it is logically inconsistent that a portion of our society make such an effort to keep our kids utterly in the dark about firearms. If education empowers us to make the best decisions under pressure, then ignorance dooms us to make the very least-informed, unreliable decisions in the worst of times. Consider the impact of education on this scenario:

Case Study: Jake Ryder
In May of 1998 a deranged student at Thurston High School in Springfield, Oregon opened fire on fellow students who sat in a crowded cafeteria. His attack was interrupted by a brave, fast-thinking wrestler named Jake Ryder who recognized a window of opportunity when the assailant's gun made a sharp click. Being familiar with guns, Jake knew it was out of ammunition and that he had scant moments to act before it could be fired again. Weaponless, Jake charged and tackled the shooter to the ground before the rifle could be re-loaded. Not only did Jake have the heroism to act, he had the knowledge to act in the smartest possible manner.

Sadly, in contrast to honest education, competing techniques have been developed by people from every corner of every issue to push public agendas on the basis of things other than fact. These techniques leverage powerful aspects of human behavior that operate outside of the sphere of logic.

Fear, for example, is a powerful motivator that feeds on subconscious emotion and works best in the absence of knowledge. As I have been up front about my position thus far, I would like to share an equally personal look at what I believe to be some of the political tools that have been disingenuously inserted into our public discourse on safety and security.

The Politics of Bans

It is human nature that when bad things happen we want to blame somebody and make them pay. Call it vengeance or righteous retribution, we humans crave our pound of flesh.

Sadly, a great deal of energy is spent after every tragedy looking for an easy out, trying to identify the one thing that caused the problem. In the case of societal violence, mountains of blame have been cast on everything from comic books and movies to video games and the internet. We are told that if we just ban these evil things, the resulting violence would go away.

Hogwash. Mankind has been relentlessly slaughtering itself by the millions long before comic books, movies, computer games or the internet ever existed.

Of equal importance, extensive history shows us that it is utterly impossible to legislate the supply and demand equation. Prisons around the world are gated, patrolled, randomly searched and watched by video cameras every minute of every day, yet they are filled with weapons, drugs and illicit devices; contraband of every imaginable kind.

Prohibition tried to ban alcohol in the U.S., creating nothing but bloody war in our streets before the ban was ultimately abandoned. For decades we have spent billions of dollars a year on the "war on drugs" but drugs are in every city and town in America. Pornography is either restricted or banned outright, yet in the U.S. alone the adult entertainment industry was estimated by an independent research firm at some $13 billion a year.

Even something as depraved as slavery is big business today. Worldwide human trafficking of women and children for purposes ranging from sexual exploitation to involuntary organ harvesting is a $28 billion a year industry that extends into the United States.

> **If there is a public hunger, no matter how grotesque or vile, somebody will rise up to feed it.**
> **Nobody -- absolutely nobody -- can stop it.**

The inability to make a ban work takes on an even more damaging tone when you realize that a national ban carries a price tag in the billions of dollars. According to the Government Accounting Office the 1994 Assault Weapon Ban cost Americans roughly ten billion dollars and produced, according to the U.S. Justice Department, no measurable impact on crime. This should beg the rational mind to ask: what did we get for our ten billion dollars?

If the answer is "nothing" then we should look for alternatives, not a second lap around the same track. As introduced earlier, that is a common sense business approach we should apply to any social challenge. The celebrated genius Albert Einstein said "Insanity is doing the same thing, over and over again, but expecting different results."

Despite this, politicians love bans because passing one takes no effort. They get to stand in front of the TV camera and claim victory because they signed a piece of paper. They know that as a society we don't track the success of a ban, nor do we hold them accountable for the money wasted. When a ban ultimately fails as they all do, the authors respond that we just didn't pour enough money into the hole.

As a matter of perspective, consider this fact about bans: during the worst of World War II citizens in Nazi-occupied Europe lived without any rights at all. Soldiers could enter any home or business, day or night, without warning or warrant and literally rip the floorboards out to look for contraband. The shipment of banned goods was punishable by arrest or on-the-spot execution. Neighborhoods and roads were crisscrossed by barbed-wire and checkpoints. Yet in the midst of that restriction, resistance movements ran veritable pipelines of weapons, explosives, medicines, forged documents and refugees. So ask yourself this; if history shows that a government with no limits to brutal force at its disposal could not make a ban work, any ban at all, then how can a government in a free nation like America ever hope to ban something?

The simple truth is, it cannot. A ban is an empty promise, a waste of money and a danger to anyone who relies on it.

The Politics of Signs

Everybody hates cancer. Our nation spends untold billions of dollars to destroy it. So what would you say if I suggested that we produce signs that read "Cancer-Free Zone" as a serious part of an anti-cancer effort? Before you answer, I remind you that the signs will cost millions of taxpayer dollars that otherwise might have helped fund clinical research for a cure. If you are like most Americans, you would probably look for the tallest building from which to hurl me... and rightly so.

How is it then that we ended up with the Gun-Free Zone (GFZ) sign as a national measure to deter homicidal maniacs? Look in the mirror and explain to yourself in simple language exactly how this was supposed to work. Our government has spent millions -- if not billions -- of dollars on the idea, so where is the logic?

Might someone have pointed out that every square foot of America had long ago been designated by law as a Murder-Free Zone, with punishments ranging from execution to life in prison? What exactly was a GFZ sign supposed to add to that equation? Was it meant to be a reminder in case somebody on a busy day forgot that murder was wrong? Did a grown-up anywhere in the process actually imagine for a moment that some armed lunatic on a mission of mayhem would even be slowed, much less stopped, by a simple sign? Were it not so tragic, the notion of GFZs would be comedic, the kind of dumb government idea you would see depicted in a movie like *Idiocracy*.

This is not meant to show disrespect to the victims of these terrible crimes, but to point out that they were sold a false promise of safety. Citizens should be outraged at having their loved ones sold a bag of lies under a label of protection.

The obvious truth is that slapping a sign on a wall is no protection at all. Only honest people obey signs. When Timothy McVeigh parked a van full of explosives in front of the Alfred P. Murrah Building to kill men, women and children, he left it in a No Parking zone. When James Holmes went looking for a theater to attack in Aurora, Colorado, he specifically chose the Cinemark theater because it had a GFZ sign so he could be confident that the patrons inside would be unarmed and helpless. The GFZ sign on that theater did not serve the public as protection, it served the criminal as a target designator.

Things like GFZ signs are pointless, counterproductive gestures shoved at us by politicians who lack the intelligence or creativity to come up with a realistic answer. It comes to us on the same level of maturity as asking felons to sit in the corner for a "time out." If you want a sobering view on the power of a sign, take a moment to interview some victims of domestic abuse and ask them to explain how a piece of paper stamped "restraining order" magically made their abusers disappear.

By comparison, have you ever wondered why we do not see shooting rampages in police stations? How many of you have laughed at the cliché movie scene in which an inept criminal tries to rob a donut shop, only to discover that the store is predictably filled with cops? The joke is the obvious stupidity -- you don't pick a fight in a room full of armed fighters.

Predators fear one thing and one thing only -- opposing force. Belief that their action will meet with swift and lethal response is the single greatest deterrent to violent crime. Yet some members of Congress tell us that putting police in public schools will never work to protect our kids. Curiously enough, these are the same politicians who surround themselves with Secret Service and Capitol Hill Police armed to the teeth with high-end military assault weapons, high capacity magazines and body armor.

Above left is a Secret Service agent-- what our politicians choose for their own protection.
At right is what these same politicians give the children of America.

To test that hypocrisy, let's turn the tables: if a GFZ sign is really good enough to trust with the lives of America's children, why don't we use them to protect Congress instead? Take a moment to write your representatives and ask them if they would be willing to trade their Secret Service details for a plastic GFZ sign and see what you get as an answer. The simple truth is that no sign or slogan can deter or defeat criminal behavior.

The Politics of Myth

Urban legends abound. We have all been amused with stories like the Darwin Awards which tell, much like the inflated parables of old, how some idiot met his untimely demise at the intersection of stupid choices and instant karma.

The highly successful show *Mythbusters* arose as a direct result of this phenomenon, to scientifically confirm or "bust" anecdotal stories like the one where a jet-assisted car rocketed off a lonely roadway like a giant bottle rocket. As any Mythbusters fan can tell you, the stories are wildly entertaining, but not all of them hold water.

Some of these myths are created by innocent embellishment, the natural way that fishing stories grow over time.[1] Others are outright lies told for reasons that are as diverse as the myths themselves.

The problem with myth is that it can get in the way of serious, grown-up discussion. Every social issue has its myths, and they are drawn like swords whenever they serve the expedient needs of one interest or the other. It doesn't matter how outlandish a lie is, nobody checks facts these days and face it, if a celebrity says it, it must be true. Right?

I had a first-hand experience with this in Washington DC at a press event held by the Violence Policy Council and Virginia Congressman Jim Moran. Delivering what amounted to a fiery sermon on the world-ending evils of a fifty caliber rifle, Moran stood in front of news cameras and claimed, with righteous certainty, that a fifty caliber rifle could knock a locomotive off the tracks. While I had been ready for a great many outlandish claims, I must admit that this one took me by surprise. Without going into a technical discussion on physics, this was as far from reality as claiming that a radioactive bug bite could actually result in creating Spiderman.

I followed that press event by contacting Trinity Rail Group, a world leader in railcar production, and asked them to comment. When they stopped laughing, which took several minutes, they first asked if a child had come up with the idea and they were stunned to hear that it had come from a member of Congress. They then very seriously explained that as a rough swag, a locomotive weighs on the order of 130 tons. They pointed out that the force of railcars simply bumping into one another day in and day out was thousands of times greater than the force of any firearm. As a matter of due diligence, Trinity tests their railcars against every sort of firearm and they noted that on impact a fifty caliber bullet simply disintegrated like a bug hitting a windshield. They concluded by stating firmly that the notion of a rifle bullet of any size puncturing a railcar, much less knocking the car off the track, was infantile.

Sadly, the media did not bother to fact-check the statement and blindly printed Moran's comment as reality.[2] I have since seen the "well-known fact" of train-flipping rifles cited in countless other articles.

No matter who is lying or why, decisions based on a lie will not produce a good result.

This phenomenon has introduced a great many misconceptions into the mindset of Americans with respect to self-defense at large. Perhaps one of the oldest and most well-known of these is the ill-founded adage that says "if you ever shoot a burglar and he makes it outside your house, drag him back inside before the police arrive." **As dumb, dangerous and illegal as this is on every possible level**, I have met countless people who assumed it as sound advice simply due to its enduring nature.

---

1   I myself have been the subject of the urban myth phenomenon, from what I take as a heartwarming perspective. I have written a number of poems in support of our troops, such as "A Soldier's Christmas" As they forward from one posting to another, I have been cited as holding just about every rank in every branch of military service, by people who are perhaps warmed by the thought that it was written by "one of us." While I love all of them and take it as a sincere compliment, when received by the next in line the assertion is accepted by fact and passed on. This is an example of how an inaccurate statement can become "documented fact" as it echoes over the internet.

2   This was just one of a dozen equally incredible claims put forth to drive public fear in support of a ban on fifty caliber rifles, which were touted as able to kill armored tanks and shoot airliners out of the sky. If any rifle had such comic book super-powers, you can be certain that the Pentagon would be handing them out to every soldier in the field. Rather than offer a sensible critique to advance their position, ban-promoters chose sensationalism and lies delivered by Moran who, because of his job, ostensibly carried a presumption of reliability.

Decisions based on "myth-information" can lead to terrible and expensive outcomes.[3] Nevertheless, political groups more interested in "winning" than in promoting the truth will routinely exploit myth as a cheap and effective way to drive public policy towards a political agenda. In an age where there is no penalty for lying and almost no fact-checking in the media, "myth-leading" is a popular strategy.

Another example of a myth put forward is that guns were invented and exist only to murder people. History tells us that gunpowder was discovered in 7th century China by scholars searching not to kill, but actually just the opposite; in the quest for an elixir of immortality. Make no mistake, once people figured out how gunpowder behaved, it did not take them long to apply those physics to throw pellets of metal at one another with murderous effect. Soon crude cannons joined the millions of swords, axes, bows and arrows with which mankind had previously been hard at work killing one another.

But as metallurgic and mechanical sciences worked to shrink cannons to fit in the hand, the power of the gun began to fill a great many other roles. It protected people from the wild animals they encountered on the trail. It allowed hunters to feed families more effectively than with the bow and arrow. Guns in the hands of police enforce law and order. Guns in the hands of victims, many of whom are smaller, slower and weaker than their attackers, drive back assaults that might otherwise be fatal.

This last point was exemplified in an adage from the Old West: "God made man but Samuel Colt made men equal." This was in reference to the Colt revolver, which did a lot to level the playing field across size, age, strength and gender. Prior to the handgun, violence exclusively favored the strong. Most women, children and the physically unfit had little to no hope at all of staving off the aggression of a larger, stronger, typically male attacker. In that scenario, a big man with even a knife or a baseball bat was fundamentally unstoppable. If we really could magically make guns disappear from the planet, we would throw society back into the dark ages where size and strength were the deciding factors in every instance of assault, rape and murder.

Yes, guns do kill people. A whole lot of people. But guns protect many law-abiding people as well. According to a Bureau of Justice study, about 62,200 people every year use a gun in self-defense against violent crime. Another 20,000 a year use guns to defend their homes and property from theft or destruction. A study conducted by Florida State University professor Gary Kleck stated that violent crimes were stopped by guns a whopping 2.3 million times a year. These numbers are hotly debated but if we assume that, like most arguments, the truth lies somewhere in the middle, we are still talking about a huge number of law-abiding citizens that became the target of a violent attack, only to survive that attack by having a gun.[4]

Myth is a dangerous and effective tool. Check your facts before you buy into somebody's story.
If the outcome of any decision is important to you, don't leave the thinking to somebody else.

---

3   In Section Two we will "bust" many of these myths and provide some smart alternatives.

4   To clarify: this does not mean that a gun was actually fired in every incident. In many cases the mere presentation of a firearm was sufficient to cause bad guys to run in fear.

The Politics of Emotion

Emotional rhetoric plays another part in the politicization of criminal violence in America. One of the most nauseating battle cries to be put forward into the debate is "No matter what the cost, if it saves just one life, wouldn't it be worth it?" It is a cry that, to my knowledge, no one has shown the backbone to challenge. Let me do so now.

I offer for your consideration the fictional tale of little Cindy, an adorable girl who suffers from some deadly form of cancer. She is the sweetest kid on the planet and at a personal level we all would give our left arm to save her. The price tag, as it turns out, is a hundred million dollars for a complex medical procedure that carries a 99% certainty of success. That's a lot of money, but hey "If it saved just one life, it would be worth it."

At the risk of sounding callous, I must point out that from a national perspective, this response is simply stupid. Yes, parents would spend everything to save their own child, but a hundred million taxpayer dollars invested into cancer research might save a thousand Cindys; it might help find a cure and end the disease forever. While it is sweet and loving and just plain nice to throw everything we have to save just one life, what do we say to the next thousand parents? "Sorry, your kid doesn't make it, we blew everybody's money on Cindy. But we saved just one life so it is OK." If you are the parent of Kid #2, this is not a comfort, this is a disaster. In fact, it is a crime.

Consider the government's own hypocrisy in this platform. School buses are some of the only vehicles allowed on the road without seat belts, despite a reported 6,000 injuries and some 20 fatalities in school bus accidents reported each year.[5] We are told that the cost to retrofit our nation's school bus fleet with seat belts is simply too high. It seems reasonable to suggest that seat belts in a high occupancy vehicle full of children would save far more than just one life; in fact the state of Alabama alone estimated that seat belts in their buses would save at least one life every year.

Oddly however, you do not hear a national clamor for seat belt installation from the "save just one life" contingent. You cannot buy a new car today without a three-point harness restraint and an arsenal of beepers and flashing lights that force you to buckle up, but we cannot afford basic seatbelts for our children riding to school every day. The standard of saving just one life doesn't seem to apply everywhere.

If we are discussing the path of a nation, we must be diligent in seeking the greatest possible good for our investment. The leaders of a nation owe that to all of its citizens. That is not an easy burden, nor will it always be a popular one.

Consider as a vivid analogy the plight of the ill-fated RMS Titanic. With what must have seemed like limitless money to spend, its builders focused on every possible amenity, every piece of bone china, polished oak and sterling silver. You could not turn around on her deck without bumping into luxury; that made people happy.

What you could not find in a crisis, however, were life boats. Amid the millions upon millions of dollars spent on frivolous opulence, the Titanic set sail with only one-third of the number of lifeboats needed to accommodate its passenger capacity. When it struck that iceberg, Titanic did not explode or sink instantly, there was considerable time to get more passengers onto lifeboats had they only been available.

Now to be certain, the boats they had saved one life, in fact they ultimately saved 710. But that fact meant very little to the remaining 1500 people who froze to death in the North Atlantic because the White Star line spent the life boat budget on pretty decorations that ended up scattered across the ocean floor. Those people died not as a result of bad driving, but poor planning and irresponsible spending.

---

5   The Relative Risks of School Travel, Special Report 269, Transportation Research Board, 2002

As a nation we are faced with the same problem today. Our national economy is in a shambles and we cannot afford to keep blowing huge chunks of money on things that don't work, no matter how cute or wholesome those items might sound. The ten billion dollars wasted on the last national gun ban could, among various things, have hired numerous additional police in every state, put security guards at every school, or improved emergency response capability to save more lives among those who are injured... the list goes on and on.[6] Armed guards might have made a difference at Columbine or Sandy Hook, but like our Titanic example, we spent money on bans and plastic signs that, as it turns out, did not save one life at all.

The phrase "If it saves one life" does not make sense if the alternative is to save countless lives. In the light of day, it is a childish, insipid and wasteful basis for a political decision. Cute, heartwarming slogans are fine for a Hallmark card, but you don't want to bet your life on one.

The Politics of Cultural Warfare

Few people, even the most ardent anti-gun activists, would put a sign in their front yard that said "We are unarmed and incapable of defending ourselves." Yet that is exactly what the *New York Journal News* did to countless citizens when they published an interactive map of all the handgun permit holders in Westchester and Rockland counties.[7] The map included permit-holder names and home addresses. The *Journal News* did this without permission, deciding for itself that the world had a right to that information.

It would be easy to imagine the outrage from the gun owners who felt their privacy invaded, but a far greater cry came first from neighbors without guns who pointed out that they had been culled out of the herd and identified as unarmed and defenseless. Victims rights groups then screamed as addresses of women and children in hiding from stalkers and domestic violence were now revealed to their abusers. Law enforcement lashed out as the map identified the homes of undercover police and corrections officers whose families immediately became the targets of criminal attack. According to the *Journal News*, their need to sell newspapers outweighed the physical and mental health of women, children, the elderly and law enforcement personnel.

With each successive day the map proved to be more and more of a stupid and reckless endangerment. Advertisers left the paper. Lawsuits were filed. Some of those victimized by the *Journal News* posted a parallel map showing the homes of Journal News employees. Ironically the *Journal News* responded by hiring armed guards. Think about that for a moment: **the people who sought to shame others for having gun permits turned to guns the moment they felt threatened.** As it so often does, hypocrisy became apparent when the tables were turned.

One is hard-pressed to rationalize a legitimate reason for such a map. The *Journal News* has not to the date of this writing explained the public "need to know" that justified its posting. By any measure it was a reckless, uncivil and ill-conceived action that needlessly jeopardized honest, law-abiding citizens and law enforcement personnel. The map was nothing more than an act of cultural malice, an attempt to "out" handgun permit holders and subject them to some form of shame or public derision in the same way that self-righteous groups of the past sought to "out" others based on differences of belief or lifestyle. Imagine for a moment if the *Journal News* took exception with a different group and posted maps of people's homes based on race, religion or sexual orientation under the claim that the public "had a right to know." We would have seen riots.

---

6   The GAO estimated a cost of $5 billion to put armed security guards in every school in America. As opposed to things like giving away billions of dollars in foreign aid, for which there is no Constitutional mandate, "providing for domestic tranquility" is in the Preamble to the Constitution and a clear responsibility of the Federal Government. Common sense says we should put our own kids ahead of the rest of the world.

7   The map was published on December 22, 2012. There is endless coverage of this across the news media.

Psychologists have long established that in general, we are less likely to harm those for whom we feel a sincere affinity. This drives one of the core tactics of hostage negotiators: to find rapport with a hostage-taker and build in their eyes a sense of sympathy for the captives. If we recognize common bonds, it becomes harder for a rational mind to inflict harm on another person.

This applies at a national level as well as for an individual one, and the impact plays into the violence we see in society. For decades now, our social perspective has slid increasingly towards division in place of unity. When we look at a group of any size we see an endless mass of hyphens. We are no longer a nation of unified Americans, but warring tribes of "-Americans." We divide ourselves with growing venom across lines of gender, sexual orientation, religion, language, social class or political view. We spend so much time focused on our trivial differences that we lose sight of what we have in common, that we are crowded together on this raft called North America facing a shared set of challenges to just survive, much less make a better world for ourselves and our kids.

Movies and television teach us the most vulgar of behaviors, with ratings driven by the quest to out-gross and out-crass the competition. Looking back, movie titles like *Jackass*, *Dumb & Dumber* and *Idiocracy* seem almost prophetic when viewed against today's society. Negative advertising is the norm at election time; seldom will you hear from candidates why they are a good choice or what they stand for; instead you will only hear smears heaped on their opponents. Tragically, the core of a winning electoral message has become "I have nothing to offer, but the other guy sucks." It is no wonder we are represented by a group that is so thoroughly unpopular and ineffective.

As our sense of unity erodes, our public behavior grows increasingly uncivil. Tantrums in restaurants and stores are commonplace, where self-indulgent patrons use any perceived slight as justification to throw food and furnishings around like spoiled infants.[8]

Voices in the public media make statements, many demeaning or blatantly threatening, that would be universally deemed repugnant if repeated back verbatim with only the roles reversed. Most people run in blind fear from the discussion but I am confident that the announcement of White History Month or a Straight Day Parade would likely end with buildings on fire. Those who shamelessly interject serious social issues into unrelated debates only harm those who actually struggle under real challenges arising from differences in race, belief, gender or lifestyle.

Along the way, merely being "offended" has become the basis for lawsuits and our courtrooms have become lotteries. Your right to free speech now ends the moment that the most sensitive person around you takes offence. Our businesses and schools are awash in HR regulations drafted to insulate them from liability arising from the most insubstantial of perceptions. One can only wonder how long it will take before somebody figures out they can be offended by somebody else being too sensitive; then lawyers can finally close the loop into a perpetual cycle of litigation.

Division is a barrier to social progress. Alienation has led to disregard and in the worst of cases, outright hatred. In a democratic Republic, fragmentation of the population assures that any measure able to survive a toxic legislative process will be an internally-conflicted brick of compromise that is least likely to serve the best interests of anybody involved. This trend has a grave impact when it applies to our national safety policy and criminal justice system.

This may sound nostalgic or idealistic, but the problems we face as a society cannot be resolved by wallowing in a quagmire of venom and divisiveness. When we give up our civility, when we become so rabid to win a fight that we cease to care who gets hurt along the way, we lose that which makes us a nation.

---

8   See http://www.youtube.com/watch?v=r9znFOdX5W4 or http://www.youtube.com/watch?v=5ywmkfRiO_Q or http://www.youtube.com/watch?v=gIVqLxPldUc for just a few of the limitless examples.

Stripping Away The Politics: Violence is a Matter of Numbers

The fallacy of the political thinking described above is the presumption that human beings will all live in peace and harmony if some outside influence is removed or controlled. It assumes that as a species we are fundamentally wholesome and kind.

We are not. Humans as a whole are competitive and violent. While our history is marked by incredible, inspiring, uplifting moments of compassion, generosity and sacrifice, those moments literally drown in the sea of ruthless carnage that makes up the rest of our story. For every life that is touched by human kindness, untold thousands are beaten, raped, robbed, starved or sold into slavery by their fellow man.

That may strike some of you like an utterly miserable view of mankind, and trust me it is no joy, but it is hard to argue with history. An estimated 100 million people were killed in the Taiping Rebellion alone. Another 70 million were killed in World War II, 60 million in World War I and the same number again for the Mongol Conquests.

As we get closer to modern time, Cambodian and Nigerian genocides in the 1960s and 70s killed some three million each, and another million in Rwanda in 1994. As this is written, the nation of Syria is reducing itself to rubble in a battle where anyone - man, woman or child - is fair game. The biggest threat to mankind is man itself.

Not all of the great slaughters of history were matters of war; religion has been quite a killer as well. In the 14th century, Aztecs massacred an estimated quarter million people every year in human sacrifice to their gods. The Spanish Inquisition brutally tortured and killed thousands to promote Catholicism. Today we routinely see innocent people bombed and beheaded in the name of Allah. Under the conviction that abortion is murder, Christian fundamentalists blew up clinics. As recently as June of 2013 the Vatican and several human rights groups stated that over 100,000 Christians are murdered every year solely because of their faith. Whatever your feelings on God may be, it is hard to imagine a Creator who is pleased with any of this.

With respect to the impact of violent media at a grassroots level, yes, we live in a world filled with bloody sights and sounds and yes, those factors may well contribute to the erosion of society to varying degrees. But before we go down that road let's take a wider look at the extent to which we have been exposed to violence over the years.

While western culture today has unfettered access to images of fictional violence, our history is filled with real graphic violence that took place in plain view, sometimes as entertainment. Public executions have been some of the largest-attended social events in history. The 1849 the simultaneous hanging of a man and woman in London drew 50,000 onlookers, a comparatively small crowd compared to the 100,000 that gathered there to watch a hanging in 1824. Those spikes you see today on the London Bridge were not put there as artwork; they were adorned for hundreds of years with the severed heads of Britain's enemies to <ahem> *make a point* about breaking the law.

Mind you, public execution is not always a matter of law; sometimes it is just for entertainment. In the glory days of Rome, Emperor Trajan held non-stop bloody games over 123 straight days that involved the slaughter of some 10,000 gladiators and 11,000 animals. Emperor Nero held games in which men, women and even children fought to the death... to amuse an audience. The Roman Colesseum is to this day considered one of the great marvels of architecture; a towering stadium where some 50,000 to 80,000 people could gather to cheer on mass murder day after day after day. In the harsh light of history, humans don't need video games or movies to teach us to kill; violence is in our DNA.

Right now, in the age of computers and digital cameras, video footage of real-world murders and executions, ranging from firing squads to stonings and beheadings, flow to the internet in real time. You can sit in your home tonight and watch the final bloody gasps of somebody blown up in Syria this afternoon. You can watch drug cartels in Mexico behead rival gang members. This isn't a one-off phenomena, it is a perpetual, up-to-the-minute flow of no-kidding murder that comes from the farthest corner of the world to a cable that runs into your living room.

Of course, if we tire of real-world mayhem, we can easily turn to movies and TV. Thanks to special effects technology, Hollywood depictions of violence are more lurid than ever. Vivid dismemberment, brutal rape and slow-motion decapitation are commonplace in popular cable programming like the award-winning STARZ series *Spartacus*. Even the History Channel's award-winning series *Vikings* centered an entire episode on an intimate, front-row seat to a grisly form of execution known as a Blood Eagle, the process of hacking through a man's ribs with an axe and pulling his lungs out while he is still alive. This is what we choose to watch for fun, at least six million viewers in the United States according to the Nielsen ratings. That puts *Vikings* atop all network broadcasting for ages 18-49.

But violence-as-entertainment goes well beyond fiction and bleeds, if you will, into the world of popular sports. Promoters can say what they want about the fine art of pugilism, but a knockout is a polite term for a cerebral concussion, a traumatic brain injury. At its core, the many derivatives of boxing and UFC/MMA is a multi-billion dollar global business based on two people entering a cage and brain-damaging each other for our amusement.[9] You can watch this in the comfort of your own home, or out with friends and family at a sports bar near you.

Given the latter examples, it might seem easy to vilify the entertainment industry *writ large* for pumping out an endless stream of desensitizing, violence-promoting gore. But in a free market society, companies only produce what the public chooses to buy. We do not see a torrent of movies where scrawny, over-sensitive leading men solve their insecurity problems with ironic quips. Those movies are typically called "Box Office Flops." Instead, we see summer blockbusters filled with explosions and gunfire because those are the movies that sell out theaters.

Consider a grotesque spectacle like *Saw*, a blood-spattered depiction of senseless torture and murder. It spawned six sequels (including one in 3D) as well as a video game... **because they keep selling out.** The *Saw* franchise has earned almost a billion dollars worldwide because from one country to the next, society lines up to buy it.

So who do we blame for that?

Much like the news media mentioned earlier, the producers of hyper-violent games, movies and print are not members of a nefarious group bent on fostering the end of civility; they are just out to make a buck peddling anything that sells. One may argue that puts them on the same moral pedestal as pimps, pushers and bookies who thrive off our other self-destructive addictions, but none of those jobs would exist without a willing and eager marketplace. If they are at fault, it is for giving us what we demand.

---

9   Sometimes beating each other to death, like the tragic last fight of Duk Koo Kim who had his brain punched apart in the ring at Caesar's palace. Unlike many people who have found theselves sprawled on the ground taking their last breaths, Kim did not hear words of comfort or sirens racing to his aid; he heard the deafening roar of the crowd. Ring sports average 5 to 15 deaths a year as the audience watches the slo-motion replay.

Of course, this is not a subject for polite conversation, not the kind of thing you bring up at the dinner table. Most people would rather talk about the best in mankind; that topic gives us hope. At the drop of a hat Hollywood brags long and loud about the impact it has on society when a movie presents a positive role model.[10] When brilliant or beautiful people wed we sincerely expect genetics to produce stellar offspring.

These happy thoughts are grounded largely in fact; role models are critical parts of our behavioral growth and genetics dictate many aspects of our physiology and psychology. Every now and then these infinite combinations align and we are blessed with a Thomas Edison, an Albert Einstein, a Beethoven, Da Vinci or a Jonas Salk -- individuals of art and science so gifted that they leave a permanent glowing mark on mankind. We often call these people "one in a million."

But as a society we ignore the other side of the statistical coin. If our population has its very best, then it has its very worst as well. We have no problems arranging people by height or weight or age; those differences are measurable and undeniable. But we are absolutely unwilling to consider that, given some sort of omniscience, the same group could also be arranged on a basis of moral fiber, intellect or the ability to behave in a lawful, social manner. If one person in a group is the absolute best on any given criteria, somebody else must be the absolute worst -- the most violent, the most cruel, the most evil. Across all of history this group is inarguably led by names like Mao Ze-Dong, Leopold II, Adolph Hitler and Jozef Stalin, all who sent millions of innocent people to their deaths.[11]

But let's put aside the apex monsters who rose to political power and look instead at the blue-collar monsters who live in average towns among unsuspecting neighbors.

John Wayne Gacy was one such monster, by outward appearance just some nondescript, rumpled schlub that people hired to be a clown at birthday parties. But behind the face paint was a deranged man who kidnapped, raped and strangled 33 young boys in his Waterloo, Iowa neighborhood, stuffing their bodies under the floorboards of his house.

Equally infamous was Jeffrey Dahmer, who murdered 17 boys **before** having sex with, and then eating, their dead bodies. Another monster named Gary Ridgeway terrorized Washington State leaving an admitted 90 women dead.

Yet as bad as they were, these monsters paled in sheer scale next to a Henry Lee Lucas or Pedro Alonso Lopez, the latter killing 3 to 4 little girls a week until a flash flood unearthed his mass grave, leading to multiple murder convictions and his confessing to over 300 sexual assaults and strangulations.[12]

In an entirely different way than Edison and Einstein, these individuals also left a permanent mark on mankind, but theirs was a stain of horror. While our greatest citizens bring life and hope, our worst leave a wake of death and despair. Evil, it seems, also has its "one in a million" individuals.

This is where statistics play a frightening role that we should all consider. One in a million sounds awfully rare until you think about the fact that the USA today is teeming with over 311 million people and world population has surged to over 7 billion. By our admittedly colloquial standard, if you acknowledge that for every million people alive, one of them is capable of unparalleled evil, we have 311 of those people living among us in the United States right now. Evenly dispersed that is over six in every state. There are 7,000 of them worldwide. So do the math: if you widen that ratio to the worst 1 in 100,000, consider the staggering number of monsters wandering our streets.

---

10   They of course vehemently deny any comparable social impact for negative role models, no matter how enticing they are portrayed.

11   Mao alone is estimated to have ordered the deaths of between 49 and 78 million people across China and Tibet.

12   Lopez was committed to a mental institution until 1998 when he was declared sane and released on $50 bail.

Today this group of monsters includes the beasts in Norway who in 2011 bombed a government building only to attack a summer camp full of kids two hours later, or the ones who decapitated 49 people on Mexican Federal Highway 41 in the Cadereyta Jiménez massacre in 2012. Another group of them slaughtered 180 civilians in churches and businesses in Nigeria on January 6th, 2012. Chinese schools have been set upon by a rash of knife-wielding maniacs who as of this writing have killed over 20 kids. As horrible as events like Columbine or Sandy Hook have been in the USA, consider in comparison the scale of the 2004 attack on a school in Beslan, Ossetia that involved 1,100 victims, 777 of them children. That crisis stretched on for three days and ended with some 334 hostages dead, including 186 kids. We have seen journalists massacred in their offices, killed over a cartoon.

This is not presented to in any way diminish one tragedy compared to another; the loss of any life is tragic. I present these facts merely to establish two things:

1) **The threat from monstrous people is global and has existed since the dawn of man.**

2) **As our population grows, the number of monsters grows as a matter of statistical certainty. More people means more violence.**

In Summary

State and Federal legislators, along with the media, are inescapably mired in politics. You know it, your neighbors know it, the world knows it. Every moment and every dollar we waste chasing political distractions, even ones that sound warm and fuzzy, will keep us from actually improving things. The measures put forward by our legislators and special interest groups are just re-runs of ideas that have failed in the past, with no new thinking, no metrics for success and no explanation as to how this time they will work as promised.

As a nation we will doubtlessly flush billions more dollars down the same toilets so legislators can claim they did something before shuffling off to collect their pension. We will with equal certainty look back ten years from now and see that the half-baked measures of today failed in much the same way they failed before. We are a divided nation and vocal proponents on every facet of the argument will hold fast to their tailored slogans and back-pedaling, fighting logic with volume, venom and blind repetition. Nobody in charge is interested in being realistic, they just want to get re-elected.

Our institutions follow suit, abdicating common sense under the banner of zero tolerance. In April of 2014 a 15 year old Special Needs student at South Fayette High School in Pennsylvania used his iPad to document the abuse he received at the hands of bullies. But when he took his evidence to Principal Scott Milburne to get help, the school responded by charging the victim with "illegal wiretapping," and pressing criminal charges. To make matters worse, the school then erased the recording before police arrived, preventing authorities from evaluating the evdience.

In the meantime our population continues to swell and by simple statistical certainty we will see violence increase in frequency and severity. If our economy continues to fall apart, stress and need will doubtlessly drive more people to crime, and some to insanity.

Our media, driven by a need to fill a 24-hour news cycle, will continue to make celebrities out of monsters,[13] feeding the delusions that will inspire other sick, pathetic losers to choose violence against the helpless as a path to visibility. Unless by some miracle we find a measure of civility and decency in our social fabric, or a leader who can unify instead of divide, the world will continue the relentless slide into abhorrent public behavior we have witnessed over the past twenty years.[14]

Yes, it is a gloomy prediction, but this is one of those points mentioned at the beginning of the book where I sincerely challenge you to look at the facts presented, put aside the politics and group thinking, and decide for yourself what is realistic. If you believe things will magically get better, put this book down and walk away.

On the other hand, if you find this assessment is accurate, then you recognize that violence in our society is a reasonable concern. In the face of any threat, common sense dictates that individuals take measures to insure their safety, just as you insure your safety against any other hazard in life. The steps you take should be based in part on how you see your chances of being victimized and how badly such an event can hit you. That is the focus of the next chapter.

---

13   As recently evidenced by Rolling Stone magazine when they reprehensibly published a photo of the surviving Boston Bombing terrorist on their cover with the glamor of a rock star. One can only hope that should the publishers or family of Rolling Stone ever have their legs blown off in an unthinkably horrific attack, that they find themselves surrounded by people who show them the same level of kindness and courtesy that their magazine showed to the victims in Boston.

14   As noted in the beginning, this is not intended to come across like some doomsday, end-of-society prediction. In fact it is merely the opposite of an unrealistic, rose-colored glasses prediction that things will magically get better by themselves. Absent a huge push, things tend to stay the way they are and the trends we have seen will most likely continue. How bad you choose to see to-morrow depends in part on how bad you see things to be today.

HOW HARD CAN IT HIT ME?

We can evade reality, but we cannot evade the consequences of evading reality.
~ Ayn Rand

As noted in the beginning of this book, the first three pillars of risk assessment are Threat, Probability and Severity. In the prior chapter we put forth a pretty solid argument that we live in a violent society and the threat of violence is not limited to urban, inner-city movie settings. In this chapter we will look at the next two criteria so we can rationally define how much effort we might expend to avoid or mitigate that threat.

The concept is rather simple: if the probability and severity of a bad event are both low, we may choose to ignore the threat completely or take only minimal protective measures. Paper cuts are an easy example; we know they can happen at any time but they don't happen often and when they do, they aren't all that bad. We could wear gloves when we handle paper, but most of us just ignore the hazard and yelp when it happens.

However, as the potential severity of an incident grows, we should become more inclined to take defensive measures. As a young man I worked a summer job in sheet metal fabrication. Imagine paper cuts inflicted by four-foot wide sheets of aluminum! Like most teenagers I waved off the urgings of my older co-workers to wear thick gloves and long sleeves, determined to suck up what I saw as the occasional nasty nick like a real man. After all, chicks dig scars, right?

By the end of my first day I looked like somebody who wrestled bobcats for a living and my pride (a young man's word for blazing stupidity) took a grudging back seat to a bit of hard-earned experience. My original assessment of the frequency with which I would bump an edge was abysmally low and the severity of the injuries in terms of pain proved far greater than I had imagined. Although no single wound was life-threatening, a dozen slices became impossible to ignore, especially amid the snickering from my veteran co-workers. A great many lessons in life are acquired when we grow tired of getting bonked in the head and learn how to duck.

In that instance, I had the good fortune of being able to survive the worst possible outcome of a bad decision. But this progression turns far more unforgiving when the potential severity of a single event can become catastrophic. Driving is a vivid example familiar to most everybody. A crash can be fatal, and we all know people who discovered far too young that speed can be suddenly lethal. The laws of physics don't care if you were unprepared to die.

This very analysis, and the fear of subsequent liability, has prompted car manufacturers over the years to invest untold millions of dollars into the development of things like seat belts, crash-absorbing frames, anti-lock brakes, safety glass and air bags. These inventions have made a world of difference to people involved in traffic accidents.[15] These changes are made by manufacturers not so much to save lives as to save themselves from very expensive lawsuits. In this forum the logic of threat-avoidance still holds true: the greater the legal risk, the more that manufacturers will spend on safety.

Now set aside the question of IF an event might happen, and look instead at the worst-case outcome. The odds of being eaten by a shark are freakishly low but in the years after the movie *Jaws* came out, many people simply refused to swim in the ocean. The mental image was so horrible that the odds ceased to matter.

To put this into practical and perhaps relevant terms, imagine for a moment that I offered to pay you twenty bucks per shot to let me fire a toy Nerf Gun[16] at you. I might miss you completely but either way, aside from the freak chance of getting 'nerfed' in the eye, it is almost inconceivable that a spongy little dart could cause you any harm at all. If somebody offered me that deal, I'd let them shoot Nerfs at me for hours. Easy money.

But what if the offer jumped to a hundred bucks a shot to swap the Nerf Gun for a .44 magnum?[17] The odds of actually being hit are probably not much greater, but the scale of injury jumps from laughable to catastrophic. For most of us the answer leaps right over "*No*" to "*Oh Hell No.*" Not for a hundred bucks, not for a hundred grand. Not even once. This is a healthy, logical response to severe risk regardless of the odds.

Estimating risk in day to day life is the great conundrum for anyone concerned about violent crime. If we knew for certain that the "one attack in our lifetime" would come at a certain day and time, we would likely pay quite handsomely for body armor and burly, armed guards. But despite a grave possible severity the likes of which we see in the news all the time, we often let our hope in a low probability talk us out of taking action. If we see a threat as increasingly unlikely, the willingness of some people to invest either time or money often diminishes no matter how severe the ramifications. Some cars are advertised on their safety record, but not everybody is willing to pay more to survive a wreck they rationalize to themselves may never happen.

So how bad can it get? Let's ask the fundamental question: **what can happen if...** you are attacked?

Some criminal attacks may be little more than a punch or rough shove as a purse is wrestled from your grasp. But even brief violence can be severe. Simply falling down can result in things like broken bones or concussions, especially for the elderly. A single knife wound, getting bashed with a brick: these over-in-a-flash events can be deadly or result in permanent disability.

Injury does not have to be the initial focus of a criminal act. In a 1993 carjacking in Ellicott City, MD, a teenager tried to throw Pam Basu from her car, unaware that Pam's 22-month-old child was in the back seat. Fighting to reach her child like only a mother can, Ms. Basu became tangled in the seatbelt outside the vehicle as the car sped away. Over the next several miles she was dragged to death. The fact that her murder was not a planned part of the crime did nothing to make Pam's last moments any easier, or her fate any less final.

---

15 Sadly there has been no breakthrough to compensate for immaturity, incompetence or impairment on the part of a driver.

16 For those unfamiliar, Nerf guns are toys that fire soft darts made of squishy foam rubber.

17 A beefy revolver described in 1971 by Dirty Harry (Clint Eastwood) as "the most powerful handgun made..."

Mind you, this is just one instance and you should not measure your own risk on the basis of a single frightening anecdote but rather on broader probabilities in your area. While statistics vary from region to region, let's look at the hard numbers on violent crime in the United States alone.

At present there are just over 311 million people living in the United States. Among them, over 5.8 million violent crimes took place in the U.S. in 2011. [18] **That is one reported violent crime every 5 seconds of every single day, non-stop, weekends and holidays included.** In the time it takes to read this sentence, another violent crime is committed somewhere in America. In the time it takes you to watch a 30-minute TV show, 360 violent crimes are committed. A United Nations study estimated that almost 15,000 people are murdered and 85,000 are raped in the US every year. A staggering 800,000 children go missing each year in America alone; that is an average of 2,185 children disappearing every single day. [19]

This violence starts early. In our schools, 56% of students surveyed report that they have personally witnessed, or have been the victim of bullying crimes in their schools, and 71% of those who repeatedly miss school state fear of bullies as the primary reason for absence. Bullies have driven fellow students to suicide, or in some cases to retaliate and murder the bully. Karma, they say, can be a real bitch.

Even at home, nearly 1.3 million women and 835,000 men are assaulted every year in acts of domestic violence. One out of every four women in America reports being raped or physically assaulted by her spouse or intimate partner. Of every three women murdered in the US, one is killed by her partner. [20] In 2013 the nation was shocked by the nanny-cam video of a housewife at home with her children, brutally beaten by a man who simply kicked in the door of her suburban home and attacked her without warning.[21]

Collectively, the U.S. Justice Department conducted a long-term study [22] and concluded that overall, 42% of all Americans will end up being victims of a completed violent crime (assault, robbery, rape, etc.) over the course of their lifetime. An additional 41% will be victims of an attempted violent crime that is somehow aborted. These two groups combined means that a stunning 82% of all Americans are expected to be subjected to at least the beginning stages of a violent crime, with less than half of those fending off or evading the attack. 52% of all Americans will be victimized more than once.[23]

The severity of violence can be both objective and subjective. In the case of physical injury there is a lot we can quantify - the number of bones broken, teeth knocked out, the number of stitches required to close a wound, the weeks or months or years required to heal. The perception of the victim however is entirely subjective. Some people fight back in the face of grievous injuries while others fall apart under the mere threat of harm. Some people weather the aftermath of a brutal attack with stoic resolve while others are left broken and traumatized for life.

---

18   U.S. Department of Justice, Bureau of Justice Statistics,Criminal Victimization, 2011

19   National Center for Missing and Exploited Children, supported by data from the U.S. Department of Justice, 2010

20   The American Bar Association and US Department of Justice, 2011.

21   http://www.youtube.com/watch?v=t4Gb9jvhHvk

22   Report: "Lifetime Likelihood of Victimization" Herbert Koppel. Bureau of Justice Statistics, U.S. Department of Justice, March 1987

23   Consider the wager that you would place if you thought you had an 82% chance of winning. Conversely, how willing would you be to get in a boxing ring if you were told you had an 82% chance of a fatal injury?

Even the briefest of attacks can be life-changing. I witnessed one such event while dining at a window booth in a town-center mall. By chance I looked up at a group of people who gathered at a curb down the block, waiting to cross the street. A young man stepped from a car with a baseball bat in hand and without a word of warning took a home run swing at a teenage girl in the crowd. She wasn't looking and never saw it coming. In less time than it took to blink the miscreant caved in the side of her head and scrambled back into the car. When I got to the scene I saw up-close what just a half-second of violence meant to this girl, who by all appearance could have been a sweet kid from any high school in America. She had not been protected by the presence of a dozen people standing around her, nor did the police magically appear in her moment of need. Whatever life this young lady had built, whatever dreams she pursued, were crushed in an instant by nothing more than a thug with a stick.

With a reported national average rate of 386 violent crimes per 100,000 people, a broad-brush swag at your odds of being the victim of a violent crime on any given day are about one-third of one percent, or one chance in 259. That might sound blissfully unlikely until you consider that your chances of being seriously injured by falling down are a very comparable 1 in 246.[24] Most of us would not think of a bad fall as an unbelievably rare occurrence; neither is violent crime. Here is a sobering way to look at it: it has been argued that you stand a greater chance of being murdered on the way to buy a major lottery ticket than you do of winning the jackpot.[25]

Violent crime is not distributed uniformly across the landscape. Factors that can influence crime rate have been argued to include population density, poverty rate and unemployment. This is not good news in today's economy. Like a great many aspects of human behavior, it does make sense that if you are surrounded by a lot of people who have little, and no means to get more, you will see more people turn to crime.

But while the term "high crime area" evokes images of run-down urban sprawls, there is growing concern among our suburbs. With the increasing virulence of class warfare, upscale neighborhoods are being put forward as bastions of the undeserving "one percenters" who are to blame for the woes of the masses. In the event of civil disturbance, there is growing concern that traditionally low-crime areas could become the focus of individual or crowd aggression. A lone criminal, no matter how big and beefy, is nothing compared to an angry mob when it comes to mindlessness.

Looking at some national statistics we see that at the time of this writing Flint and Detroit, MI sit at the top of the list of violent cities, followed by St. Louis MO, Oakland CA and Memphis TN. At the other end of the spectrum, citizens in Maine, Vermont and New Hampshire enjoy the lowest crime rates. When you look at your own risk, you should take into account where you live and the trends that are affecting your local economy. As you read this, an online search for "FBI list of most dangerous cities" should provide you with the most up-to-date geographic breakdown of urban America.

Given these statistics, it is curious that so many people who are otherwise safety-conscious choose to ignore the risks of violent crime. I have asked this question countless times, in discussions and training sessions, and the most oft-repeated answer is "It is a scary subject; I just don't like to think about it."

I challenge the accuracy of this answer, even if the speakers believe it to be true at the moment. Yes, the notion of violent crime is ugly and frightening, but so are a lot of things we face in life and still cope with rather easily. We do not dwell on the ghastly mental image of burning to death when we put batteries in our smoke detectors. Parents don't visualize the graphic details of electrocution before popping child safety covers on our wall sockets.

---

24   Both stats from the National Center for Health Statistics and the National Safety Council data, 2011

25   While this statement is admittedly anecdotal as presented and subject to debate as to the size and participation rates for a given lottery, the odds of winning a 2012 Powerball jackpot were estimated at roughly 1 in 175 million. Even such rare events as being killed by lightning are estimated by the National Weather Service at 1 in 3 million. That is a long way from a mere 1 in 259.

If you think about it, few things in normal life can compare with the visual horror of a bad car wreck, and every time we get in a car we roll our dice against the odds of being in one of over 10 million traffic accidents that collectively kill around 35,000 people a year, in this country alone but most of us smile while making "buckle up" a consistent, positive routine for our kids. By comparison, the notion that crime is uniquely "scary" just doesn't hold water.

The difference, I believe, boils down to the certainty of physics versus our perception of human choice. We know in our heart of hearts that fire will not change its course to spare our lives, it will burn us without thought or hesitation. We cannot tell ourselves the high voltage line will have pity and give us a break, or that we might catch a lucky bounce if we fall off a tall building. The very idea would be idiotic.[26] Mother Nature is heartless when it comes to breaking her laws of physics.

When it comes to crime, however, many people con themselves into believing that the rapist will take pity, that the murderer will discover a golden heart, that the awful people who have killed and maimed their way through all of history will at the very last moment see the light of human compassion when they get to me. That is an equally idiotic notion, like expecting gravity to flinch or a Great White shark to turn away out of sympathy.

Human violence can be every bit as remorseless as nature, and far more cruel. Fire won't study you from a distance, learning your behaviors so it can attack when you are most vulnerable. Gravity doesn't take delight in making people suffer for as long as possible. Humans do these things all the time, and much worse. Of all the species on the earth, humans can be the most senselessly vicious and inhumane.[27]

The first step in being better prepared is to accept that there are people out there willing and able to hurt you. No, it most certainly isn't fair; decent people lead quiet respectful lives and don't deserve to be raped, assaulted or murdered. Decent people shouldn't get kidnapped and held prisoners in basements for years of rape and abuse. Decent people shouldn't have to carry weapons or learn how to fight; many of them are not particularly strong or fast or very good at all the security stuff. A lot of them walk through life rather oblivious to their surroundings, increasingly nose-down in a smartphone swapping text messages with a friend. "After all," the decent American asks, "why would anybody want to hurt me?"

Violent criminals have a name for decent people like that. *Easy meat.*

I understand this is a crummy outlook, and I don't offer these facts to frighten or depress you, but rather to make another important point. Criminal violence is a statistically documented phenomenon that threatens everybody. Sadly, that group includes you and your family.

But wait, you say! Is it not true that a relatively small percentage of repeat offenders are a big part of the problem? Why don't we just keep them locked up when we catch them the first time?

---

26   Mind you, idiots are a powerful tribe and the internet is brimming over with self-made videos of numbskulls who light themselves on fire, skateboard down concrete stairs or try to leap over speeding cars only to suffer the all-too-predictable gruesome effects of physics. Such idiots are exemplified by the likes of David Villalobos, who in 2012 reportedly jumped from an elevated monorail into a tiger enclosure at the Bronx Zoo to, in his words, "be one with the tiger." The only surprise is that he survived, although severely injured, proving once again that the sole legacy of some lives may well be to serve as a warning to others.

27   It is impossible to bring to these pages descriptions of just how vicious humans can be to one another. Let it suffice to say that Hollywood characters like Hannibal Lecter are pale, watered-down versions of very real killers like Pietro Pacciani, William Coyne, Albert Fish or Andrei Chikatilo, monsters whose real crimes could never be shown on the bloodiest of movie screens. A Google search for these names may well keep you up at night.

And a damn fine question that is. A U.S. Justice Department study reported that roughly 70% of all violent criminals arrested had prior arrests for violent crime, over half of them being felony level crimes.[28] A separate study concluded that half of the inmates in local jails were out on parole or probation at the time they committed their latest offense and 40% had served at least three prior incarcerations to include violent felonies.[29] Logic suggests that if we kept them locked up after the first violent crime, we could cut the violence back dramatically.

But if you noticed, we slipped into a "why" question that ultimately, we cannot answer. Your guess is as good as any expert's as to why our government releases violent criminals time and time again. We are told it is too expensive to keep them jailed, but the cost to society for letting them out seems far greater. We are told it is cruel to keep a criminal locked away for his violent choices, but we ignore the cruelty these monsters inflict on innocent men, women and children when they are released again and again. What we know, with mathematical certainty, is the terrible outcome of early release, yet we do it endlessly. The only conclusion one can draw from this pattern is that the criminals are more important to our politically-blinded government bureaucrats than are the law-abiding victims that suffer as a result of this catch-and-release program.

So, if we put aside the why, we are left with the unavoidable fact that we do let criminals go and will continue to do so no matter what the outcome.

**Any expectation that our system will protect us,
through deterrence or confinement, is simply unfounded and unrealistic.**

In Summary
Violent crime does not touch everybody. How much time and energy you expend on your defense should take into account your surroundings. The odds that you or someone you know will experience a violent crime first hand are statistically significant. If a violent crime occurs, even brief in duration, the effects can range from minor to lethal.

At this point, those who oppose a self-defense mindset will say "that is why we have police" as a reason to dismiss all concern. In the next chapter we will examine the strengths and limits of police protection and if we can expect the cavalry to come running in our moment of need.

---

28   Brian A. Reaves, U.S. Department of Justice, Bureau of Justice Statistics, Violent Felons in Large Urban Counties (2006), available at http://www.bjs.gov/content/pub/pdf/vfluc.pdf.

29   Doris J. James, U.S. Department of Justice, Bureau of Justice Statistics, Profile of Jail Inmates, 2002 (2004).

WHO WILL SAVE ME?

"Superheroes were born in the minds of people desperate to be rescued."
~ Jodi Picoult, The Tenth Circle

Every day police officers don body armor, uniforms and pounds of equipment before taking to the streets to make the world a better place. They approach strange cars at night with no idea if the occupant has a weapon in hand. They enter buildings, charge down alleys, follow signs of violence into every dark corner that their training, experience and common sense would otherwise tell them to avoid. They do it to stop Bad Guys[30] from doing harm to a person they have never met.

Sadly, unlike *Star Trek's* Captain Kirk, police don't have teleporters that beam them from place to place in the blink of an eye. Police don't have the psychic powers depicted in *Minority Report* that allow them to pinpoint a murder before it happens and be standing by, cuffs in hand, to prevent the heinous act. To come to your rescue, police have to drive through the same snarled traffic and crummy weather that you face every day. I've met cops with the heart of Superman, but not one of them had X-ray vision or the ability to fly.

Let's think about what that means to you.

Day in and day out we Americans go through our lives largely unobserved by police; most folks like it that way. Those who obey the law appreciate privacy as a benefit of being an upstanding member of society. Even if we have nothing to hide, we really don't want an officer watching us all day, peering in our windows, following our cars. That is, until we need help desperately. When our tires hit a patch of ice and we slam into a tree, we want a paramedic to appear before we bleed to death. When our house is on fire we look for firefighters to carry us out before we burn. When a jogger finds herself tackled into the bushes by a monster ripping at her clothes, she wants a cop to appear - not in ten minutes, not in two, but right now.

---

30   Men and women both commit violent crimes but as I have no interest in cumbersome references to call out all possible combinations of whatever gender, transgender or sexual identity issue might be important to somebody, I will simply use the terms Good Guys and Bad Guys to refer in a general sense to law-abiding citizens versus the criminals that prey upon them.

So when it comes to a rescue, how fast is fast enough? Statistically, the average violent crime is over in three minutes or less. Many common attacks like muggings, rape and street robberies can be over in moments. Hollywood has sold us the idea of protracted fisticuffs but in reality it just doesn't take very long to beat, stab or shoot somebody.

Justice Department studies conducted decade after decade show that the large majority of these crimes are committed not with guns or bombs or sophisticated weapons but instead with everyday, on-hand items like hammers, kitchen knives, a steel pipe, a brick or even an empty fist. But neither brevity nor the medieval nature of the weapon is any barrier to physical, mental or emotional injury. As mentioned earlier, something as commonplace as a rock can inflict horrific, life-changing injuries in the blink of an eye.

Case Study: Reginald Denny

In 1992, trucker Denny was driving an 18-wheeler through Los Angeles when a riot broke out. Denny had no involvement with the riot, he was just a guy stuck in traffic trying to get on with his life. That did him little good when protestors dragged him from his vehicle and beat him with junk in the road; a broken piece of medical equipment, a claw hammer and a chunk of concrete. The attack lasted only one minute, but left Denny with a skull fractured in 91 places. Even though TV helicopters were broadcasting the event live from the onset, police did not magically appear to stop the gruesome assault.[31] Mr. Denny was left with a permanent crater in his head and impairment to his ability to speak and walk despite years of rehabilitative surgery. One minute can echo for a very long time.

In his celebrated Theory of Relativity, Albert Einstein postulated that both time and space would stretch if you could move at the speed of light. While we may not experience velocities like that, we have all seen how our events around us can affect our perception of time. A beautiful day may pass in the blink of an eye while time spent stuck in bumper-to-bumper traffic can feel like an eternity.

Just how quickly our sense of time can change was the focus of an old bar-room test of toughness typically embarked upon after the volume of alcohol exceeded that of common sense. In this challenge competitors poised their hand palm-down a couple inches above a lit candle to see who could hold out the longest. For most folks, the first few seconds would pass without notice but as that tiny point on the palm quickly grew hotter, the perceived gap between seconds stretched dramatically. Many a tough guy found a span of mere seconds to become unbearable. In cases of assault, a single cut in the wrong place can lead to exsanguination -- bleeding to death -- in a few short minutes. The difference of minutes or even seconds can take on an entirely new meaning when your blood is leaking out.

This leads os to the term Response Time, which refers to the seconds, minutes or hours that pass between your making a call for help and someone actually arriving. While a simple concept on its face, Response Time is something most people don't fully understand or appreciate. As this can be critical to your planning and safety, let's break the process down into three critical phases: Notify, Locate, and Respond.

---

31   Four citizens came to Mr. Denny's aid after the attack was over to render aid; their courage and kindness were credited with saving Mr. Denny's life.

Notify

Have you ever had somebody ask "where were you when I needed you?" only to have you point out that no one told you there was a problem in the first place? That relationship applies everywhere, especially in times of emergency. Aside from the rare luck of a heroic and capable bystander who stumbles upon you by sheer chance, if you have a crisis you will not likely see a bit of help until somebody, typically a 911 operator, is told that you have a problem.

Now you can make this call, or somebody else could place the call for you. But what happens if that call is never made? Unlike sports or game shows, violent criminals will not give victims a "two-minute warning" prior to commencing an attack, nor will they knowingly allow you to "call in a lifeline" like some TV game show. Keeping you away from a phone is actually one of a violent criminal's top priorities.

Conditions unrelated to the crime itself can make matters worse. If there is no cell coverage where you are, you may not be able to call for help even if you have the time.[32] The same logic applies to a cell phone with a dead battery. Natural disasters do not consciously target you personally, but large-impact events will often knock out or overload the phone systems all across the affected area. Absent a stroke of epic good fortune, it will likely be a great challenge to call anybody for help during an attack or sudden disaster.

> **No matter how bad an event you are suffering,
> your response time does not even begin until you notify somebody.**

Locate

If you have never heard a frantic 911 call, it can be very unsettling. You hear the sound of people in the grip of pain and fear. You hear people cry, scream, swear, pray, sometimes you hear them plead for their lives. On the worst calls you hear them die. It is impossible to put into words the helplessness a 911 operator feels hearing somebody in dire trouble with no clue as to where to find them.

Locate is the second critical step in securing help. It is one thing to get a 911 operator on the phone and shout "He's trying to kill me" but if you are not calling from a land-line -- which may provide a physical address automatically -- police may have no magic way to know where you are. It is up to you to quickly and accurately convey your location so responders can come to your aid. A clear head and a degree of situational awareness are vital in communicating this type of information.[33]

Respond

From the instant that police and emergency response units know your location, they will send the entire cavalry charging to your rescue, right? That is a nice thought, but life doesn't always work out that way. Responders may be engaged with other rescue efforts already in progress, or may be a considerable distance away. If your emergency is of a disastrous nature, the impact of that event may well bring traffic around you to a standstill or make roads impassible altogether.

---

32   One of several reasons that so many crimes are committed in places like underground parking garages.

33   Simple steps to an effective 911 call are covered in Section 2.

Worse yet, in our mis-managed world, budget shortfalls may mean your 911 system is under staffed and unable to respond at all. Imagine being on hold with 911 listening to a recorded message about the importance of your call.

This is not a joke or exaggeration. In 2013 Oregon citizens were shocked to find that their 911 system was, in the words of Governor John Ktzhaber, suffering its own state of emergency. Josephine County Sheriff Gil Gilberson said "There isn't a day go by that we don't have another victim," blaming budget shortfalls for the persistent inability to fight crime. His summary: "If you don't pay the bill, you don't get the service." In the process of this longstanding crisis the Sheriff's department issued the following suggestion to the county's 80,000 or so residents. "You may want to consider relocating to an area with adequate law enforcement services."

Let's look at how these factors play out elsewhere. In bankrupt Detroit, response times to a 911 call are running at just about one hour. In more functional settings, as reported in *American Police Beat* magazine, a 2010 study on response times showed that in Atlanta, a major metropolitan city, it took on average 11 minutes and 12 seconds between the receipt of a high-priority 911 call and the arrival of an officer at the scene. This matched almost to the second the response times seen across the country in El Paso and Kansas City. Oklahoma City came in at just under 10 minutes while Nashville scored just below 9. As a normal matter of business, the Los Angeles Fire Department has the goal of a six-minute response time for medical emergencies, but according to a November 2012 *Los Angeles Times* article the LAFD failed to hit that mark roughly 85% of the time.

When you consider these statistics, remember that on national average, **most violent crimes are over in less than 3 minutes.**

So what does this tell you? Well, if the crime is over in 3 minutes and officers won't arrive for 10 in a best-case scenario, **you are on your own for the duration of the attack** even if you get to make a complete 911 phone call before the attack begins. Your ability to survive may be the sole factor that determines if the officer arrives to find that an assault has taken place, or a murder.

That may shock you. Most Americans grow up with the belief that "it is the job of police" to rescue us before we are harmed. Sadly this is not the case, practically or officially. This fact is recognized from the level of local police policy all the way up to the Supreme Court. In the case of *Riss versus New York*, 21-year old Linda Riss sought police protection from her estranged lover, Burt Pugach after he made overt threats that included statements like "when I get through with you, no one else will want you." True to his threats, Pugach hired three assailants to throw a corrosive chemical in Linda's face, leaving her permanently scarred and blind in one eye. Despite her repeated prior attempts to secure police protection from a specifically-identified assailant and a clear threat, the Supreme Court ruled that the police had no legal obligation to provide what it termed "special police protection" and that the police could not be held liable for criminal action even if there was reasonable forewarning that it would take place. A key point of the case relative to this discussion was set forth in the Plaintiff's argument:

> "What makes the City's position particularly difficult to understand is that, in conformity to the dictates of the law, Linda did not carry any weapon for self-defense. Thus by a rather bitter irony she was required to rely for protection on the City of NY which now denies all responsibility to her."
> ~ *Riss v. New York*, 22 N.Y.2d 579,293 N.Y.S.2d 897, 240 N.E.2d 806 (1958).

Riss is hardly a unique case; there are numerous examples from around the country which all follow the same theme.

> "Law enforcement agencies and personnel have no duty to protect individuals from the criminal acts of others; instead their duty is to preserve the peace and arrest law breakers for the protection of the general public."
> ~ *Lynch v. N.C. Dept. of Justice*, 376 S.E. 2nd 247 (N.C. App. 1989)

"...a government and its agencies are under no general duty to provide public services, such as police protection, to any particular individual citizen..."

~ *Warren v. District of Columbia*, 444 A.2d 1 (D.C. App. 1981)

Recognizing this fact, municipalities such as Milwaukee have gone as far as producing Public Service Announcements encouraging citizens to buy a gun and learn to use it so they can defend themselves while waiting for police. In one such PSA Milwaukee County Sheriff David Clarke Jr. states that "personal safety is no longer a spectator sport." He points to the growing impact of fiscal cutbacks as yet another factor reducing the ability of police to respond. Sheriff Clarke elaborates:

"With officers laid off and furloughed, simply calling 911 and waiting is no longer your best option. You can beg for mercy from a violent criminal, hide under the bed, or you can fight back. ... Consider taking a certified safety course in handling a firearm so you can defend yourself until we get there." [34]

Critics of Sheriff Clarke suggest that he is advocating vigilantism or "auditioning for a Dirty Harry movie" but there is nothing in his statements to even remotely suggest either. Based on the inescapable facts, Sheriff Clarke is simply acknowledging established Supreme Court precedent and the impact of fiscal reality on the ability of any municipality to protect an individual. Instead of feeding his citizens a meaningless political promise, he is giving them honest and dutiful advice likely to enhance their day-to-day safety.

That kind of integrity is a rare quality these days and should be applauded. Nonetheless, critics have attacked this honesty as being politically incorrect, but political correctness never saved a life or stopped a rape. Sheriff Clarke's guidance -- urging citizens to get training on the safe and effective handling of a defensive tool -- is sound and well-balanced, supported by the very logic presented in this book. Consider this: the alternative is to do nothing in the face of danger and simply accept the consequences. That choice is certainly open to anyone, but it seems like a pretty lousy course of action.

For a moment, let's set aside the negative dynamics caused directly by a criminal and look at some of the other factors that may be important if you find yourself looking for help.

Response Capacity

Most hospitals operate at or above 95% maximum capacity every single day. "On the verge of overload" is a normal condition. This is largely driven by business realities; a hospital cannot afford to keep an entire floor of empty beds staffed and ready just in case a disaster strikes.

But what does that mean when even a minor disaster takes place? In many communities across the country an event as small as a multi-vehicle traffic accident can overload a hospital Emergency Room. In the face of any sort of mass-casualty event, hospitals often have to re-direct patients to medical centers all across the region.

If this can happen with a minor overload, what happens when dozens, maybe hundreds of people are involved? What happens when an event like a storm or blackout impacts the hospital facility itself, or the staff that works there? Who will come running to help you in the wake of a hurricane when some portion of the police, firefighters and paramedics may understandably choose to care for their own families first? And what happens, as it almost always does, when government officials fail to utilize the scant few resources actually on hand?

---

34   http://www.foxnews.com/us/2013/01/26/wis-sheriff-urges-residents-to-get-gun-training/#ixzz2JJY42ip0

This scenario was vividly demonstrated in the wake of Hurricane Sandy in 2012. Given names like "Frankenstorm" and "the perfect killer" by meteorologists for days in advance, Sandy grew to be the largest Atlantic hurricane ever seen, measuring some 1,100 miles across. Sandy was no secret; everybody knew she was going to be terrible. Within a pretty well-defined set of parameters they knew when and where she would strike.

On October 29, Sandy slammed into the Eastern Seaboard, centered on New Jersey and New York. Severe damage was widespread and injuries were everywhere. Between New Jersey and New York alone some 3.5 million people were left without power, many in homes with roofs or walls torn apart. One would think that this was the end of the horror story, but it was just the beginning. Now humans got involved.

When volunteer electrical workers from Decatur, AL arrived to help restore power, they expected harsh conditions like cold and flooding. What they did not expect was to be pelted with debris thrown by members of the local electrical workers union who violently opposed assistance, even free assistance, from a non-union state. As one might expect in the face of inexplicable violence, the volunteers packed up and went home, leaving the powerless residents of New Jersey to huddle in the cold. In times of crisis, humans can be their own worst enemy.

In New York, authorities had two massive generators in place to power the media tent that was set to cover the New York Marathon, with a third back-up generator standing by. It was estimated that two of these generators could have provided power to 400 homes in blacked-out Staten Island, but they were never released to provide aid. They sat idle while people shivered in the cold. Similarly, food service trucks had been standing by to drop off hundreds of cases of bottled water along the race route, but these were not re-directed to families left without running water.[35] Government officials had plans and back-up plans in place to support a TV-covered race, and little in place to support citizens left cold, hungry and homeless by a known-well-in-advance disaster.

The inability or unwillingness of our own government to help us goes all the way up to our nation's Congress. While legislators dragged to the last minute a vote on avoiding the fiscal cliff in 2012, they refused to even bring up the issue of Hurricane Sandy relief, choosing instead to go home for the holidays. With no relief after sixty-six days of suffering, New Jersey Governor Chris Christie publicly referred to these national legislators as "toxic." Christie said that the indifference to such immense suffering shows "why the American people hate Congress."[36] This assertion seems to be supported by most national polls that reflect a very dim view of our legislators.[37]

Keep in mind, I do not point this out to promote or bash one party over another. What I do point out, and I think is beyond argument, is that nobody in America can rationally expect a government-led relief effort to swoop in and save us from anything. There may be heroic, wonderful, brilliant people scattered throughout our government who really care, but collectively these people are crippled by a sea of mindless bureaucrats and conflicting regulations that have reduced our system to gridlock. If you strip away all emotion, that is the harsh reality we see every day.

35   Abuse of Power, New York Post, Nov 2, 2012

36   http://politicker.com/2013/01/chris-christie-says-lack-of-sandy-relief-shows-why-the-american-people-hate-congress/

37   Mainstream pollsters such as Gallup report that Congress in 2012 earned the lowest-ever recorded approval rating, averaging less than 15% across the year. While decidedly less scientific and less serious, a Public Policy Poll in 2013 suggested that Americans rate Congress below lice, cockroaches and traffic jams, and only slightly above North Korea, the Ebola virus and Lindsay Lohan. One quote stated "Lice are crummy, but at least you can get rid of them."

In fairness, I submit for your consideration one additional factor that contributes to our government's inability to do anything affirmative, and that is our litigation-addicted environment. In America you can be sued at any time, by any one, for any thing. We have all seen the celebrated cases of idiots who race to the lawyers after being injured by their own stupidity; those who sue because icy sidewalks are slick, or because hot coffee is hot.[38] In April of 2014 national news covered the aftermath of a traffic accident in which Sharlene Simon, driving her SUV, reportedly struck and killed 17 year old Brandon Majewski as he rode his bicycle. Following the tragedy, Simon filed a million-dollar lawsuit against the family of the boy she killed, claiming that he was an "incompetent bicyclist" whose death apparently proved to be emotionally disturbing. Nothing, it seems, will soothe a troubled mind quite like suing the grieving parents of your victim. But beyond all boundaries of common sense or decency, anybody can be sued for any reason. If there is a pimp or pusher for every lurid appetite, there is a lawyer standing by for the most reprehensible cases.

But more relevant to a discussion on self-defense is that individuals and institutions can and do get sued for actions taken in an effort to help people in need. Despite the presence of various Good Samaritan laws created for just such a purpose, doing anything to help somebody in need can result in a lawsuit from very victim you tried to help.[39]

As a result of all this litigation, institutions move towards tighter and more restrictive rules -- not to make it easier to save somebody but to make it harder for the institution to be sued. The fear of a lawsuit for a botched CPR attempt doubtlessly drove the Nursing Home policy of non-intervention referenced earlier, in which a nurse then refused a 911 operator's instruction for her to perform CPR on a dying patient.

That same fear drove the 2013 decision of Wal-Mart regarding stock clerk Kristopher Oswald after the young man came to the aid of a woman being assaulted in the store's parking lot. Although six or seven other employees stood and watched, Oswald put himself at risk and saved the victim from further harm. Sounds heroic, right? Sadly, heroism isn't Wal-Mart policy and he was fired immediately. When every civil human instinct tells us to help somebody in need, company policies around the nation unflinchingly say "let them die" because getting involved will undoubtably result in a lawsuit. Let's take just a moment to look at just one of these litigation-avoidance phenomena and see how it works.

Zero-Tolerance Policies (ZTP)

The logic of a ZTP runs like this: if you make a strict rule, and eliminate all chance for common sense to come into play, you can consistently fall back on "I was just following orders" no matter how bad the outcome.[40] Unfortunately, school ZTPs can produce ridiculous and dangerous outcomes as you can see in news items from the first quarter of 2013 alone:

---

38   These suits run well into the insane: in 1991 Richard Harris sued Anheiser-Busch for false advertising resulting in emotional distress as well as physical and mental injury because drinking beer did not make him "lucky with the ladies" like the guys on the TV commercials. In 1996 physical therapist Paul Shimkonis sued a Florida strip club for physical and mental anguish suffered when a stripper's breasts "hit him like cinderblocks" during a lap dance. The list is endless.

39   It comes as no shock that a vivid example comes to us from California, where the court in the case of Alexandra Van Horn vs. Lisa Torti ruled against Ms. Torti, who dragged Ms. Van Horn from a severe car wreck she saw as being in imminent threat of fire. Ms. Van Horn sued her savior under the assertion that being dragged to safety aggravated her injuries. The court said that citizens have no duty to help one another and that choosing to do so comes with an exposure to liability.

40   A stance known to those with a sense of history as the Nuremburg Defense. It didn't hold up well then either.

- A 6-year old girl in a South Philadelphia elementary school had a single piece of folded notebook paper that reminded a school administrator of a gun. The administrator yelled at the little girl in front of the class for bringing a gun to school in violation of the school gun free zone policy.

- A 5-year old girl in Mount Carmel, PA laughingly told another child that she was going to "shoot" her with a pink *Hello Kitty* soap-bubble toy. She did not actually have the toy in school. A teacher suspended her from school stating that the mere mention of a "bubble gun" toy was a violation of the school's zero-tolerance gun policy.

- A 7-year old boy in an Anne Arundel, Maryland school was suspended on a formal weapons charge because a teacher thought his half-eaten Pop Tart looked like a gun.

- A 6-year old boy was playing Cops & Robbers with his friends during recess at his Maryland elementary school and pointed his index finger at empty space in the process of arresting an imagined desperado. School authorities suspended the boy, saying that his extended index finger was a violation of gun policy.

- A 7-year old boy in Colorado was off by himself playing soldier when he made a throwing motion towards some imagined enemy entrenched in a sandbox. The boy was suspended from school on a weapons charge for... and I am not kidding... possessing an imaginary weapon.

These instances are not novelties, they are tragedies perpetrated by adults with no grasp on reality, adults who feel empowered by blind rule to bully little children. These cases have resulted in innocent children having school suspensions and real-world weapon charges placed on their record with potentially huge implications for the rest of their lives.[41] Kids have been publicly humiliated and traumatized at an age where few can even grasp the concept of violent intent. In the case of the Anne Arundel incident, the school board re-affirmed the decision insisting that the child carry for life the stigma of a formal gun charge on the basis of a half-eaten Pop Tart.

People making these types of deranged decisions are incapable of mature thought and should never be entrusted with the safety of children.

Psychologist, family physician and author Dr. Leonard Sax said "These zero-tolerance policies are psychotic, in the strict sense of the word: psychotic means out of touch with reality." People who cannot distinguish a real-life danger from a half-eaten pastry cannot possibly be counted on to make a responsible decision if an actual threat presented itself.

Ask yourself, what did a teacher think a 6-year-old child was really going to do with a Pop Tart, regardless of its appearance? Can anyone articulate a shred of rational concern as to how this child might have gone on a pastry-wielding rampage? How exactly was an "imaginary hand grenade" going to cause harm? Instead of bringing an adult perspective, a tiny handful of school personnel across this country inflict shame, embarrassment and trauma on children in the furtherance of their own delusional priorities or rabid politics. These zero-thought policies empower the most insipid and brutish individuals to wield autocratic, life-changing power with impunity. "I was just following orders."

---

41   Imagine trying to explain, during a college admission process or job interview, why you have a weapons violation on your record, much less make your reviewers believe that it was just a soap bubble or a Pop-Tart.

As stated earlier, the easiest way to illuminate hypocrisy is to reverse roles of the players. Lets put that to the test: ask yourself what would happen if parents of one of these students filed identical weapon charges against the same teacher for having a staple gun on their desk? What about the endless supply of caulk guns, grease guns and spray guns used to maintain the buildings, bus fleet and landscaping? If a pink plastic *Hello Kitty* bubble gun is a firearm by explicit definition, certainly these other items qualify as well. If the need for a Zero-Tolerance Policy with no exceptions is so severe that we saddle kindergarten children with criminal records, should it not apply to everyone with equal brutality? The moment we hold school employees to the same standards applied to students, the discussion would change dramatically.

The simple fact is that ZTPs have no place in a thinking world. Our children deserve the guidance and protection of thinking adults. If there is anything we as a society should not tolerate, it is pretentious, unthinking bureaucrats who put half-baked rules and personal politics ahead of common sense and the safety of our children. If you have kids in school, you should find out if they have Zero-Tolerance Policies in place on any subject[42] lest some inadvertent gesture or imagined object result in equally mindless suspensions and criminal charges being levied.

In Summary

What should be extremely clear by now is that we face real threats from criminals and we can expect little help to magically appear if one of those threats rises up in our face. The proactive and reactive policies in place in our institutions favor absolute, unthinking rule over common sense, and it is no surprise they have proven to be ineffective and poorly applied. Some people making decisions about our children's safety cannot distinguish imaginary weapons from real ones and they should be removed from those responsibilities. The Supreme Court has stated that our safety is not the obligation of law enforcement, and the police themselves in many cases urge citizens to provide for their own defense while governments, schools and companies publicly punish citizens who try to help themselves or one another.

On the strength of those facts, it is time to look at what we can do to protect ourselves. That takes us to Section Two.

---

42   And there are many that go beyond weapon rules. In 2012, Colorado eight-grader Breana Crites suffered an asthma attack during gym class at Lewis-Palmer Elementary School. Fortunately, Breana's friend Alyssa McKinney, a fellow asthma sufferer, shared her identical inhaler and staved off a possibly deadly situation. The school responded by suspending both girls on drug charges, despite opposition of both parents who saw the act as heroic and life-saving. Consider the abhorrent lesson for kids to follow: let your classmate die or you will be punished.

IT ALL STARTS WITH A PLAN

"If you fail to plan, then you plan to fail."
~ Benjamin Franklin

A recipe for a cake, a script for the school play, an architect's drawing; no matter what you do in life, things work out better if you start with a plan. This chapter will define the terms and concepts that shape a simple yet solid defensive plan tailored for your life.

Simple is an important point. A good plan should help you enjoy your day-to-day life with little active thought, expense or effort. On one hand we don't want to go through life fretting about the proverbial monster in the closet. On the other hand, most people do not respond well to sudden stress for which they are unprepared. Many a bad incident has been followed by a victim lamenting "oh I wish I'd thought of that..."

A simple plan can give you the comfort of knowing that if the closet door were to open unexpectedly in the middle of the night that you are ready to run, to survive, or if need be, to crack the monster in the head with a baseball bat. A plan can pay off big in times of crisis, but merely knowing you have a plan can pay off every day in peace of mind.

Professional security plans are typically complex documents, involving terms we've mentioned before, things like vulnerability assessments, risk mitigation strategies and contingency plans. Let's strip away the jargon and look at the process in simple terms.

Most of us have others we care about, either by choice -- friends and family -- or by way of professional responsibility such as students or employees. Your group may be as small in number as one, say a spouse or child. Others, like a school principal or building security executive, may be responsible for the safety of hundreds, even thousands. For the purpose of simple reference we will call that group your Circle, as distinct from the rest of the population around you, aka the Herd.

Nature teaches many lessons about the interplay between predators and prey. We all love to watch that dance play out on the Discovery Channel; we marvel at the slow-motion footage of the tiger running down the gazelle or the shark suddenly appearing out of the darkness with gaping jaws to munch the hapless seal. There is no more vivid metaphor for violent criminals. The moment we let go of why humans would attack and simply accept that they do, we can look at them in the same clear light as we would for any other predator in nature.

Think about a shark. If you were fishing and saw a huge grey fin slide through the water, would you choose to jump out of your boat?[43] The very idea gives most sane people the shivers. Yet every day people park their cars down in dark, unmonitored garages or go jogging down unlit paths, ignoring the predators we know to frequent these environments. They see the fin and jump in the water anyway.

For the purpose of a consistent analogy for the remainder of this book, let's cast members of our society against familiar, in fact rather iconic roles from a North American forest. If you will indulge this bit of stage-setting you will see how these roles are applied throughout the strategies presented thereafter.

Wolf

Wolves are predators, meat-eaters. They survive by killing and devouring other animals. They can hunt alone but are exponentially more deadly when they hunt in packs. They may have a non-threatening, disarming appearance until they show their fangs. Wolves do not understand human concepts like pity or mercy.

Sheep

Sheep are the staple diet of wolves. Sheep are dull and slow and largely oblivious to their surroundings. They survive as a species not by saving any given individual, but simply by breeding faster than the predators can kill them off. Survival is based on sacrificing one for the good of the herd. Sheep represent the portion of our population that plod through life with their noses buried in a smartphone or tablet, oblivious to events taking place around them.

---

43   Mind you, it has been done. In 2014 Shaun Harrington, armed with nothing but a small parakeet cage, decided to try this trick with a deadly tiger shark in a "Jackass" stunt that nearly cost him his life. Fortunate to survive, Mr. Harrington later described the event as "not the smartest thing to do." He has a gift for understatement.   http://www.youtube.com/watch?v=PGzJtD4CUH8

Rabbit

Like sheep, rabbits are a tasty treat and have no real ability to fight back, so they rely on speed to stay off of the dinner menu. Given that fact, rabbits have to remain very aware of their surroundings. In a race for survival, a head start on either side can define the outcome. Thankfully for rabbits, they need only be faster than the sheep.

Bear

Bears can live among the wolves with little fear of being attacked. By comparison with sheep or rabbits, bears are powerful and well-armed. Bears are also easy for the wolves to recognize and it is rare that a wolf will go out of his way to pick a fight with a bear.

Chameleon

Seldom recognized for the tasty treat they really are, chameleons change their appearance to hide from notice, or to look like something more dangerous. Typically lacking the speed to run or the firepower to fight, chameleons take advantage of everything that wolves have learned about other deadly species. If you cannot be poisonous, the strategy goes in nature, then at least look poisonous. As long as the wolf avoids you, the net result is the same.

Turtle

The turtle is neither fast nor powerful, in fact it is one of nature's most timid creatures. Yet despite their inability to run or fight, turtles don't fear much from the wolf either. If attacked they just bunker down in their nearly impenetrable shells and suffer the indignity of being rolled around until the wolf gets weary and leaves them alone in favor of easier prey.

Now most people can effortlessly accept these characterizations in the context of nature and understand instinctively the nuances between them. We do not doubt for an instance what will happen to the rabbit should he daydream while the wolf closes in, nor do we expect that sheep will heroically group together to overwhelm a pack of wolves by force. Sheep scatter in fear and a clueless rabbit gets eaten. Science tells us that these roles and behaviors have evolved over millions of years and billions upon billions of violent attacks where the prize for second place was a center seat on the dinner plate.

The rules of survival in nature apply to us as well. These strategies represent various combinations of the "Four Fs": Feign, Fortress, Flight and Fight. They exist as listed in an ascending order of preference.

Feign [fān]   verb
Pretend to be affected by (a feeling, state, or injury): "he feigned a limp".
To simulate, sham, dissemble or fake.

Feign is the art of the chameleon and whether or not you might think so, we have all feigned at some point in time. When you know your buddy is about to ask you to help him move this weekend, you painfully flex that sore back you just remembered. You feign when you happily chow down that last bite of some awful meal because somebody made it for you with love. There are many polite or selfish reasons we may choose to project a different truth, and some good safety reasons as well. **Just as we can feign to be less than we really are, we can feign to be more.**

How we appear can have a significant impact on being targeted by a criminal. A 2004 Department of Justice study determined that 64% of all violent crimes committed against females were committed by somebody intimate with the victim, meaning somebody who had the opportunity to observe the victim in his or her day-to-day life. So what exactly do we say with our day-to-day choices? Do we appear capable or helpless? Do we blend in with the crowd or stand out?

Let's begin by looking at the notion of camouflage, the art of blending in to one's surroundings to avoid being noticed by a predator. Like chameleons, there are *Phasmidia* -- bugs that look just like twigs -- who are also masters at this game. In a military context, snipers are called upon to move unseen through hostile terrain without the support of a protective herd. In a game of hide-and-seek played at a live-or-die level, they have refined the art of blending in with their environment to the point of near invisibility.

But hide-and-seek is largely an all-or-nothing gambit. In the case of a home intrusion, for example, hiding under a bed may provide simple camouflage, but if you are spotted, the jig is up and the bed provides no further protection. This is where the other side of Feign comes into play, giving off visual cues that suggest you are not the weakest member of the herd. Remember, you don't have to be the fastest, you just don't want to look like the slowest and weakest.

Your choice of attire and posture can say many things about you and most people love the notion of expressing themselves in a free society. But out on the street some choices of attire can say things we may not prefer. Expensive jewelry, for example, might single out one person from a crowd as a rewarding target. High heels may be stunning but they say "slow runner." Walking nose-down in a smartphone says "oblivious to surroundings." A jogger with no visible cellphone may be dragging along a sign that says "can't call for help." Those may strike you as unkind interpretations, but that is how criminals look at their prey. The next time you are out in public, look at the people walking around you and ask yourself, which ones could you beat in a race, in a fight? See what details about their physique, attire or behavior affects your evaluation. That is exactly what a criminal does.

This is where Feign comes into play. Many harmless creatures that cannot hide from view have adapted to appear like something more dangerous than they are. In most cases, it is easier and more effective to appear unattractive as a target than it is to be invisible.

The Hog Nose snake is a ninja of imitation. While harmless in real life it can impersonate a cobra's wide hood, shake its tail in the manner of a rattlesnake or flop over and play dead. Any one is a reason to leave it alone. Combined, these behaviors are often enough to give a predator reason to steer clear or lose interest.

Feign tactics typically do not rely on factors like strength, speed or fighting ability but they do require a tiny bit of specific forethought and planning. Feign is a game of mental manipulation and the tactics of Feign can be applied on top of any other strategies you may wish to keep as alternatives. This strategy requires only a tiny bit of effort and does not preclude any other option.

Case Study: Police Feigns
Law enforcement routinely uses the psychology of Feign in a reverse direction. An armed, uniformed officer can in most areas walk down the street with little fear of sudden attack. When an officer enters a crime-ridden area, the Bad Guys may just scatter like cockroaches. As a result, police are sometimes called upon to disguise themselves as the weak and helpless, going to theatrical lengths to appear like ideal victims in areas where serial predators operate. From choices in clothing and posture to demonstrable lack of awareness, their goal is to give off every observable sign that they are alone, clueless and defenseless. While this is a danger to the officer acting as bait, the tactic has been an extremely successful tool in capturing violent criminals by leveraging the Feign psychology. How you look and act can wordlessly draw criminals in or push them away.

So where is your game of Feign played? Anywhere you live, work and play. Somebody who is observing you in your workplace may well have the opportunity to see your office or desk, or may see the car you drive. Look at the following photograph and put yourself in the shoes of a predator on the hunt: do you see anything that might cause you to prefer one person over another?

Think like a Bad Guy: stick figure families are everywhere, but to a sex offender this cute little image reads "single mom with two small kids and no dog." If your car sits in a driveway at night, it tells the world -- and every predator out there -- where you live and who is inside the house. This is the reverse of feign; it is advertising your vulnerabilities on a 24-7 basis.

Our cars are a big point of observation. Every day they sit unattended where a Bad Guy can amble up, look inside, and scan the surroundings with nobody watching. If the car is covered with, for lack of a better phrase, "girly" decorations, a sexual predator might reasonably conclude that the owner is female and bound to return to this location. Without even being there the owner may have displayed signals that draw a predator to wait and watch.

Awareness is a legitimate tactical requirement and you will appear less vulnerable simply by keeping your head up and eyes open. Periodically scan left and right as you walk. Even a passing glance at a reflective surface such as a store window can provide you a rear-view mirror as to what may be following. When possible, keep your strong hand[44] free. While incredibly subtle, these tiny actions are visible to somebody who stalks humans for a living. They are the signs of someone who is likely to be be harder to surprise and harder to handle. It is critical to remember that criminals are typically not pressed for time; they will let one potential victim after another pass by until they find somebody who seems to be the most oblivious, the most incapable.

A house can project its own image as well. A dark house with overgrown landscaping affords a trespasser greater freedom to move about unseen. Keeping shrubs and trees cut back around windows means that somebody inside can more readily see what is going on outside. Exterior lights, especially motion-sensitive lights, can prove very uncomfortable to somebody trying to probe a house for an open door or window. Signs that suggest a dog in residence, or an alarm system in place (even if neither is true) can give a burglar cruising the neighborhood an excuse to go to the next house. Just a small bit of effort or investment in your residence can go a long way towards making it seem less vulnerable.

Keep in mind, Feign is the art of illusion and you should cheat shamelessly. You do not need to actually take a karate class to buy a one-dollar bumper sticker at the local dojo. You do not need to own a dog to hang a Beware of Dog sign on the fence or leave a large dog bowl outside the back door of your house, but you can readily imagine what either sight would cause a stranger to think.[45] You do not need to own a gun to wear a Smith & Wesson ball cap or a military service T-shirt.[46] Things around your home or office speak about you even when you are not there.[47]

Displays such as these all raise a measure of unease in criminals lurking about, predators who constantly run their own "what if" analysis. "What if I jump her and she really is a black belt?" or "What if that old guy used to be a Marine?"[48] That is precisely the sort of doubt you want to plant in the mind of someone sizing up your ability to fight.

---

44   Your predominant hand, right if you are right-handed and vice versa. This is the hand you will be most capable with should you need to react defensively and having it encumbered makes you appear more vulnerable.

45   Big dogs are a big fear for most burglars. For bonus points on this Feign, go to the local pet store and buy one of the largest raw-hide chew-toys they have. Loan it to a friend with a big dog and let him mangle it up. Then set that next to the bowl by the back door and you send a very compelling message. Attention to detail is a powerful storytelling tool.

46   Be aware, in today's society this can create risks in certain environments. In April 2013, Jared Marcum, a student at Logan Middle School in West Virginia, was suspended from school and arrested for merely wearing an NRA t-shirt even though it did not conflict with school policy. In a practical sense, Freedom of Speech is no longer equal.

47   I was first introduced to this idea years ago by someone who had a small plaque in her office that read "First Place" in a defensive pistol competition. She had not struck me as the gun-type and when I asked her about it she chuckled and said she wasn't; she had the plaque made at a local engraving place. Twenty bucks, she argued, gave everybody who walked by something to think about. It was a brilliantly subtle ploy I will never forget.

48   The latter clearly written in the voice of the unwashed criminal who fails to recognize that once a Marine, always a Marine.

Case Study: Bishnu Shrestha

In September 2010, retired Gurkha soldier Shrestha was on a train to Nepal when a gang of some 40 armed criminals attacked the passengers, robbing many and attempting to rape an 18 year old girl. The gang gave no thought to Shrestha until he unexpectedly burst into their midst with his Khukuri (a distinctive, heavy-bladed knife), killing three Bad Guys, wounding eight and driving the rest from the train. Stolen loot abandoned by the fleeing brigands included 200 cellphones, 40 laptops, copious jewelery and over $10,000 in cash. Although severely wounded in the process, Shrestha said after the fight, "Fighting the enemy in battle is my duty as a soldier. Taking on thugs on the train was my duty as a human being." While an extreme example of heroic response from an unlikely passenger, this type of surprise is the basis of fear among criminals every time they contemplate an attack.[49]

Understandably, for some people the words and icons they display have immense philosophical value. It might feel like some sort of ideological betrayal to display a message or symbol you do not personally espouse. That choice, like any other, is personal and yours to make.[50] But if you want to exploit every advantage to reduce your exposure to crime, there are few things you can do that are cheaper, easier, less expensive and less risky than Feign to change how criminals view you.

Risks and Rewards of Feign

Feign offers the greatest possible ratio of gain versus cost in terms of time, effort or money. You only need to give a Bad Guy one good reason to pass you by, to have one plausible fear for his own personal safety in order to affect his decision-making process. He is desperately looking for the easiest target - so don't be that target. To do this you only need to appear less like prey than those around you.

Lastly, a Feign does not diminish your ability to shift to any of the subsequent strategies when necessary. There is no downside to appearing more alert and more capable.

---

49 Pause for a moment and consider the difference of culture. After the above incident Shrestha was hailed as a national hero and refused a cash reward offered by the girl's family. In Michigan, Walmart employee Kristopher Oswald was fired for stopping an assault on a woman in the store parking lot. Florida lifeguard Thomas Lopez was fired by his employer, Jeff Ellis & Associates, for saving a drowning man who was outside his defined zone. In New York, British plumber David Justino fashioned a tourniquet and saved the life of a woman who had her foot torn off in a traffic accident, only to get the sack from Bass Plumbing & Heating for "attracting too much media attention." No act is so noble or so obviously right that it cannot result in termination, lawsuit or criminal prosecution.

50 As a personal example, even though it would likely suggest I had an affiliation with a brutal, violent culture capable of fighting, I would not wear or display a Nazi emblem for any measure of safety.

Fortress ['fôrtrɪs] noun
A place of refuge or support.

What happens if we become the active focus of a criminal? It may happen because we are in the wrong place at the wrong time. We could be at home when a burglar breaks in or in a theater when shooting suddenly erupts. Maybe we are just walking across an empty parking lot when some guy steps out of the shadows with a knife.

If Feign is off the table, your remaining choices in order of preference are Fortress, Flight and Fight. Each one will demand increasingly more from you in terms of physical capability and each will expose you to greater overall risk. Each one will likely play out in a progressively shorter window of time within which you will have to react. You may consider and reject one or more of these options in the blink of an eye, but the priorities remain. Before we examine the options in running or fighting, let's consider the lesson of the Turtle.

The premise of the turtle is simple: when threatened you simply pull inside your fortress, lock the doors and wait for the predator to get bored, exhausted or frustrated enough to leave. If your fortress is strong enough you can wait for help to arrive no matter how long that takes.

Unlike a turtle, most citizens do not haul a mobile bunker around wherever they go. This doesn't mean it cannot be done to a limited degree; some members of our society employ a highly mobile aspect of the Fortress strategy -- body armor. Once considered a spy-movie staple, developments in arid fiber technology and other material science have made body armor a standard item for police across the country. While police officers do all they can to avoid being shot at, or at least avoid being hit, body armor provides one last layer of partial defense against the bullet that strikes home. As you will see, the same materials that protect police are commercially available in backpacks and garments for civilian use, with very distinctive strengths and limitations.

But body armor is not really a refuge, nor can it be expected to hold out for longer than it takes a Bad Guy to aim for your head. By comparison, one might argue that a car or truck is a type of mobile fortress and in truth an average car can provide some degree of physical separation. But much like body armor, this is at best a partial option. Glass windows are not designed to stand up to physical assault and the ability of a stationary vehicle to provide long-term fortification is limited.[51] The real strength of a vehicle is to provide a measure of protection while outrunning or running over the enemy.

So what makes a good fortress? Sailors have an old saying, "Any port in a storm" that is truly wise in this context. In a crisis a Fortress can be any space which you can enter that an opponent cannot, or into which the Bad Guy cannot project force. Stepping into something as common as a stairwell or closet and bracing the door with anything available, including your own body if you have to, can enhance your ability to hold off some types of physical attack.

The strategy of Fortress has the most obvious applications for home security, the term itself drawing on the adage that your house is your castle. Fortress can be a very solid way to survive the time it takes for help to arrive.

This strategy places almost no demand on your physical condition. The Fortress does most of the work. It does, however, encourage at least a brief emphasis on planning to select or create a space in your home that cannot be readily breached by force. You may consider the entirety of your home to be your Fortress, or restrict your focus to a single interior room that may not have vulnerabilities like glass windows.

---

51   A vehicle's mobility, on the other hand, can have immense impact on the safety equation. Remember that distance between you and any threat is always an improvement.

At the high end of Fortress-building there is an established industry providing "Panic Room" design and construction that can turn almost any space in your home or business into a highly reinforced keep. These rooms may contain a small supply of food and water[52] as well as a first aid kit in case somebody gets injured en route to the sanctuary. They may have separate phone lines or access to video cameras so those inside can monitor events in the rest of the house. The cost for such a Panic Room is limited only by the imagination.

But at a basic level, your Fortress may need little more than a solid wood door with a deadbolt lock. A bedroom with such a door can prove a daunting or at least time-consuming barrier. Other small enhancements like an extended security strike plate can multiply the durability of the door and the doorframe.

Anything employed to further strengthen or reinforce the "shell" of a Fortress room can also be a benefit. While formal Panic Rooms may have expensive metal-clad or concrete walls beneath a cosmetic covering, those building or remodeling a house can readily add additional lumber or brick filler between the studs of normal stick construction to "up-armor" what might otherwise just be drywall over foam insulation.

Expectations for a Fortress room must be realistic. Reinforced wood construction may stand up to a lot more abuse than the flimsy, hollow-core doors typically found in home interiors, but neither will stand up forever against someone with an axe. Wood construction is also limited in its ability to defeat bullets, although one would benefit considerably from forcing a Bad Guy to fire blindly through a wall as opposed to allowing him into your room where he can aim.

In a pinch, a Fortress effort may simply be taking ad hoc advantage of any secure space you can enter that denies entry to the Bad Guy or any other destructive force.

Case Study: The Oklahoma Bank Vault
The most dramatic example of the latter took place in Moore, Oklahoma in May 2013 when a devastating tornado dropped out of the sky. With only moments to act, twenty-two bank employees took to the vault as the tornado struck. In the wake of the storm the vault stood intact while the entirety of the bank building around it was reduced to splinters.[53]

Admittedly, few of us have a bank vault handy, but any room can provide some measure of protection from a human opponent. A sizeable object like a dresser or a file cabinet can help block an inward-opening door and create additional barrier against force coming through the wall.

There are risks associated with a Fortress strategy. From the onset there is always a risk when you enter any room that has no escape route. In a perfect world your Fortress should have a back door, an avenue of escape you can use if you see that your front door is failing.

---

52 Which may be as little as a few Granola bars and a can of soda or bottled water; something to provide comfort should an event drag out for several hours. Medical conditions that demand timely intake of specific foods or prescription medications should be considered when packing an emergency cache.

53 http://www.dailymail.co.uk/news/article-2328837/Oklahoma-tornado-2013-Bank-customers-employees-rode-tornado-inside-vault-thats-left-standing-building.html

Professionally designed panic rooms can provide for alternate exits that may use stairs or ladders to allow escape on a different floor. If you plan to take refuge in an otherwise inescapable Fortress, you should consider two planning points: how to best harden the front door[54] and how to give yourself a better fighting chance if that door fails.[55]

Fortress does depend on a small edge in terms of reaction time; you must get inside your Fortress before the Bad Guy gets to you. Once again, this is where planning can come into play. If you hear something troublesome like breaking glass or the proverbial bump in the night, your first reaction should be to at least drift towards your Fortress. The closer you are to refuge when danger reveals itself will reduce the time it takes to get inside and shut the door.

A modern, professional-grade "safe room" or "panic room" is very straightforward. Prior to being cosmetically hidden, the room is simply a solid box built as threat-resistant as desired. When you consider that normal 2x4 and drywall home construction can be penetrated with a fist, a space wrapped in an extra layer of plywood, cinderblock or poured concrete can provide considerable added protection. A solid-core door with a deadbolt lock, or interior door-bar, makes a formidable barrier. Doors hidden by wall mirrors or bookcases add a layer of concealment; a Bad Guy can't assault a fortress he can't find.

---

54   The term "harden" simply means to make something tougher to break. A hard target is tougher to hit and more resistant to damage. Be it materials like wood, brick, stone or metal, every bit of solid stuff you put between yourself and a Bad Guy is more stuff he has to get through to reach you.

55   As discussed later in this book, force can act as a barrier if you consider the ability of force to stop a Bad Guy from reaching you. The ability to project disabling force at an intruder may provide additional protection if preceding physical barriers are defeated.

Today, inexpensive closed-circuit TV cameras are available as kits online or at everyday stores like Wal-Mart. Some offer wireless setup that require little more than batteries to activate. Some will even stream to your smartphone. As a bonus, night vision technology allows cameras to see in the dark better than you can with your own eyes. This is a tool that is ideally suited for a Fortress scenario. A nondescript camera outside your bedroom, for example, can stream video to you as you move into your Fortress. From inside you can observe other parts of your home or yard with no exposure, in fact without revealing your presence at all. If someone intrudes, you have a huge head start to get inside your Fortress. If instead you find that the crash downstairs was caused by the cat you have only to step back out, grumble at the cat and clean up the mess.

There are a few things you might want to keep inside a designated Fortress in the event of an actual emergency. A phone charger is one essential, as your phone likely represents your only contact with the outside world. Water, especially in the summer, can be important if you are stuck inside for any duration. Things like snacks or a blanket are not likely "survival level" needs but may provide a measure of creature comfort in what could be a stressful time. A first aid kit and a fire extinguisher are two good items to keep handy in your home and a designated Fortress is a good place to keep them. You should also think about any prescription medications you might need on a daily or hourly basis. Just a handful of simple items can make a world of difference if you find yourself locked in a room for a few hours.

A Fortress may be a good place to keep a suitable weapon of choice. This is one scenario that highlights the difference between a gun and any other class of weapon. Faced with somebody beating their way through a solid door, a gun arguably offers the greatest ability to project force from within a confined space.[56]

Keep in mind that a Fortress door may not fail all at once. If a Bad Guy has kicked a hole in your door he may reach inside to unlock it, or stick his face in the hole to see where you are.[57] While a frightening visual, from a tactical perpective this is a significant opportunity. Inflicting severe injury on a limb or face may be enough to drive off or disable an attacker. In such an instance, you have the option to strike whatever target you are given with the most damaging weapon you have and keep hitting it until it goes away.

Risks and Rewards of Fortress
On the good side, a successful Fortress response can postpone your need for more risky endeavors like running or fighting. Lock the door, call for help and wait.

On the downside, a Fortress with no "back door" can become an inescapable dead end if the "front door" fails. This may be mitigated to some degree by the fact that the bottleneck of the front door will force the Bad Guy to advance through a defined area. If you are left with no recourse but to fight back, that bottleneck can provide some tactical advantages.

---

56 As discussed in the story of 12 year old Kendra St. Claire, presented later in this book.

57 Hollywood fans might recall the infamous "Here's Johnny" scene from *The Shining* where a crazed Jack Nicholson sticks his face through a half-shattered door while Shelly Duvall stands just a foot away clutching a 10-inch carving knife. Had she been think-ing, the movie would have ended right there.

Flight [flīt] noun
The act or an instance of running away; an escape.

Imagine that the day has gone very badly; you find yourself the focus of a criminal attack and have no safe refuge in sight. Only two choices remain, the most fundamental two choices in all of nature: Flight or Fight. For some, it is time to channel your inner Rabbit.

The strategy of Flight is easy to understand: run like hell. There is no way to predict how far you may have to run; Flight ends positively when you reach some refuge, assistance or public venue that deters further pursuit, or when the predator just gets tired and gives up. Flight ends badly when the predator is faster.

The first thing to keep in mind about Flight is that random panic-stricken running may lead into a dead end or into the path of unrelated dangers like traffic or a bad fall. People have dashed away from a mugger only to run headlong into the path of a truck.

If your basic nature is to run when danger pops up, you would be well served to follow three simple "Rabbit Rules":

Rule 1 - Cardio[58]
Staying in shape will help you be a better runner when running is most important. Even routine walks will provide a health and fitness benefit that can improve your speed and endurance.

Rule 2 - Dress for success
When you are out on the street, choose footwear that is comfortable for running. Athletes do not compete in high heels for a reason.

Rule 3 - Be observant
Awareness of your surroundings can play two important roles in a sudden flight scenario. The first will tell you when you need to start running and the second will tell you which way to go. When you enter an area, take just a moment to scan for exits. This is especially true in cases of crowded venues that can turn to chaos if people panic. Be prepared to use non-traditional exits; if a fire or fight broke out in a restaurant, your fastest way out may be through the kitchen or a window.

If you are betting your life on a race, cheat to win. Pulling anything into your wake can impede a pursuer. Anything you can do to clutter your tracks may force an attacker to trip and fall or to swing wide to avoid an obstacle. If a Bad Guy is fixated on you, leading him into hazards like potholes, curbs or ditches, or into the path of moving vehicles can suddenly interrupt his ability to give chase. Running tunnel-vision into traffic is a bad outcome for you, but luring your violent pursuer into the front grill of a speeding bus is a better outcome than getting assaulted or having to fight for yourself. When you hear a loud crunch you can think "Say hello to my very large friend."[59]

---

58 Yes, fans of the movie *Zombieland* just chuckled, but the advice is spot-on.

59 This may sound flippant but I saw traffic leveraged to perfection one night on a sidewalk near Nathan's Famous Hot Dogs in Fort Lauderdale, FL. A teenage boy was accosted by several older thugs who made it clear they meant to do him grievous harm. Recognizing he was outnumbered with nowhere to go the boy abruptly shoved the closest thug. It was not much of a shove, but unexpected and just enough to get the Bad Guy to take two good steps off the curb into fast-moving traffic. The taxicab did the rest.

If in the process you do hear the proverbial thump or scream behind you, keep running until you reach a place of refuge and call for help. Never turn back towards an assailant even if you believe he has grievously injured himself. You have no legal duty to render aid to somebody who tried to hurt you; leave that to the authorities. Do not consider yourself safe until police have secured the scene.

There is a group dynamic that affects Flight scenarios and you should exploit it as readily as do animals in nature. Herding is the tendency of non-fighting animals to gather and move in groups. Alone, an animal is a singular point of prey. In terms of Feign you cannot appear less attractive than the other guy if there is no other guy, nor can you have somebody slower than you to serve as easier prey. Some predators may be deterred by the sheer presence of others. If more people are present there is a greater chance that one may be a fighter or may be able to call for help. Traditional predators want situations they can control and the fewer victims in one place, the better.

Herd movement has many applications, but the most obvious is parking lot scenarios, especially in multi-level or underground parking facilities. If you are leaving a restaurant, mall or theater you may find that the bright sunny parking lot you parked in earlier has become a dark, gloomy place. Walking alone means you are the most attractive target of opportunity and given their size, the exit from the parking facility may be a considerable distance away. This is where herding can be a big benefit. If you are alone and need to enter a dark or out-of-sight area, pause in a populated area until a group is heading in your direction and walk along with them. Most malls have security personnel and many restaurants have valets or doormen; as a rule these people will be willing to walk you to your car if you ask them. At the greatest extreme, call a cop. If you feel a situation is dangerous, do not hesitate to ask an officer for help. Most cops would rather escort you and have a positive encounter than show up to find you injured or dead.

You should be aware, however, that the herding paradigm changes in rare events like suicide attacks and bombings. There criminals seek to catch as many people as possible within the lethal radius -- the area within which they believe their actions will cause the most harm. The more people crowded around a bomb, the greater the number of casualties. But as simple crime by definition is common and bombings are rare, statistics say that we are safer in groups.

If you think about it, avoidance is simply proactive Flight. It is moving away from potential danger before it becomes an active threat. If you move early you don't have to rely nearly as much on speed; in fact walking away from a potential threat is far better than having to run from it after it has bared its teeth. Any effort you make to add distance and barriers between yourself and the unknown will increase your odds of escape if it suddenly becomes a threat.[60]

Staking your safety on flight can be challenging if you are not very mobile, or when you are with others that you cannot leave behind, like a child, an elderly parent, or someone on crutches. The slower you are, individually or as a group, the more you need to emphasize awareness. To complicate this process, predators may be immoral but they aren't all stupid; they often choose attack sites to specifically limit your flight options, like alleyways, elevators and underground parking facilities.

---

60   Consider the events of the Boston Marathon Bombing. One victim testified that he watched the bomber place a backpack on the ground and walk away. Anybody who has been to an airport has heard time and again about the dangers of unattended baggage, yet the victim stood in place next to a then-abandoned backpack until it exploded. Had he simply walked away, a tactic which worked just fine for the bomber, he would have reduced his exposure to injury.

Risks and Rewards of Flight

Flight is largely an all-or-nothing strategy; either you get away or you don't.

On the positive side, a successful flight means you do not have to incur the hazards and injuries of a fight.

On the negative side, running is strenuous work that may leave you winded or possibly injured if you trip or fall. Being hurt or out-of-breath can degrade your ability to fight thereafter. If you do not believe you can successfully escape an area you may wish to run towards a place near you that increases the chance you will be seen by others who may render aid or at least call for help, or run towards a location that favors your odds in a fight.

Fight [fīt] verb
To attempt to harm or gain power over an adversary by blows or with weapons.
To defend against or drive back a hostile force.

It is often said that force never solves anything. I respectfully beg to differ. Force, or the threat of force, is the underlying basis for every contest of will on this planet. Before you get up in arms (the irony of that statement being somewhat intentional) consider for a moment that diplomacy and society exist as a means of avoiding force. We are polite to one another, even under severe agitation, because the abandonment of politeness can lead to violence. But when one party ceases to be polite and resorts to force, no amount of right, reason or logic can physically stop him.[61] The only thing that can stop a resolved, determined force is greater force. It is simple physics.

It is also said that might does not make right; at further risk of being inflammatory, I must again throw the challenge flag. Right, as opposed to wrong, is a very subjective position. When two armies clash, both carry the belief that right is on their side, that they fight in the name of truth, that their cause is just. Both cannot be correct. Ultimately, one army will get slaughtered and the other will write the history books. The winner is always right.

Dare we take this argument to a theological level we would find argument that right and wrong are divine absolutes handed down by God. But might is at the center of that divinity; if you oppose God you go to Hell for all eternity. God is right because God has the biggest stick. Depending on how you choose to look at it, might may or may not make right, but it most certainly makes reality.

These two points are offered to put aside the distraction of your being right or wrong when it comes to being attacked. **Being right doesn't matter** when a brick is coming at your head. Being fast matters. Disabling your opponent as abruptly as possible matters. If you want to be right, live to write the history book.

In this day and age, fighting is arguably the least desirable course of action. This is not stated on the basis of some desire to embrace all mankind in love and reason, it is because fighting exposes you to a hundred ways to end up getting screwed.

- Even the most lopsided physical contest can produce the most unlikely or unexpected outcome.[62] You can lose what looked like an easy fight, you can cause injury to somebody by mistake, you can be mistaken for an assailant and find yourself at the wrong end of misdirected justice from the next person who walks up. Every fight is a crapshoot.

- A fight of any duration is almost certain to leave all participants injured to some degree. This may be injury inflicted on you by an opponent, or injuries you receive when striking them or colliding with something solid around you. Many a fighter has walked away having defeated an opponent, yet suffering broken knuckles or other wounds. This may be less, in some cases far less, than the injuries you might have otherwise received, but the point remains valid. Violence exacts a price from everybody involved.

---

61   The fashionably academic flaunt phrases like "the pen is mightier than the sword." It is a prosiac thought with lovely historic implications, but in a practical sense the axiom is a lunatic statement; you can imagine how such a fight would end. In a time of physical conflict, words are just vibrations in the air that cannot block a punch or deflect a weapon. Words are mental and emotional tools that have no physical power.

62   Consider the parable of Goliath, a giant of a man purportedly some nine feet tall. Clad in full armor, he must have felt like a tank when he looked down at tiny David and chuckled "What the heck does that little kid think he's gonna do with a slingshot?"

- Any time you use force against another human being you risk hazards of potentially severe infection if they bite, bleed or spit on you and transmit diseases like hepatitis or HIV.

- You run an increasingly severe risk of lawsuit or criminal charges if the force you employ harms somebody else, even a person from whom you are defending yourself. One day far removed from your fight a group of jurors may sit in a complete vacuum and decide that your response was not appropriate to the risk you faced. As we all saw in the George Zimmerman case, politics and the media can throw incredible weight into the workings of the judicial system.

In some instances you can see a fight coming, like the loudmouth jackass who tries to talk you into taking the first swing. But others will come at you sideways, out of the dark. Those are the dangerous ones, the opponents who have a goal and a plan to achieve it. In those cases you will have to react as best you can to actions that will likely unfold rapidly and without warning. Criminals who choose to attack will likely have had some opportunity to observe you and assess your apparent physical firepower. They will pick the time and place to put you at the greatest disadvantage. They will attack when they are convinced they will win. That decision may ultimately be in error[63], but the cost to everybody of proving the point is undefined and unrestricted.

In a purely legal and medical context there is no winning a fight; you will never end a fight better off than you were before your life entered that scenario. Success in that context is measured in terms of how well you minimize the degree of injury and liability you incur. I wish there was some sort of yardstick, some basis of measure that I could offer. Do you knock a guy's teeth out to keep your wallet? Do you use enough force to potentially kill a guy to stop a rape? Nobody can answer that for you, that is a personal thing. I have met people who have a sharp clear line backed with powerful conviction about right and wrong, what they will or will not tolerate. There are others who say they could not harm another person even to save their own life. You live or perish with your own choices.

In a practical sense, however, fighting is not about retaining what you had before the threat appeared. Every risk of emotional or legal nature, when lumped all together, may in some cases pale compared to the harm you can suffer by not fighting back. This is notably true when somebody tries to force you into a vehicle to take you to an undisclosed location (known in police parlance as a Secondary Crime Scene). **The level of personal danger associated with being moved by force cannot be overstated; once hidden out of sight, away from help, your prospect for survival is dismal.** There is no book that can tell you when and how events might unfold but consider for a moment this common assault scenario:

You are walking alone in a parking garage when you find yourself accosted by three very unsavory individuals who announce in the most vulgar of terms their intention to beat, rape or kill you. Maybe all three. You may not realize it but your life has already changed; what happens next is just a matter of deciding how and in what form your injuries will play out. There is no future in which you walk away physically, emotionally and legally unscathed.[64] You may win the fight handily only to carry a lifetime of legal scars. What you do in that instant may well decide if you walk away at all, with whatever injuries you may incur, or be found broken and dead when police arrive. It may decide if you keep your home and your dreams. That may sound really bleak, but that is the reality of a serious fight and why you should do all you can to either avoid it or finish it on your terms.

---

63   A frankly hysterical example of this appears on YouTube when a young lady on an elevator is attacked by a taller thug, only to respond by unexpectedly beating the living hell out of him and sending him scrambling for his life in utter panic. http://www.youtube.com/watch?v=5VX7gc9HyYE

64   If you prefer, think about it like the long horrifying slow-motion moment when your car slides out of control on a rain-slick highway. You may hit the oncoming truck head-on but if you act fast, you might clear the truck and slam into the trees on the far side of the road. Neither is good, but you will fight like mad to avoid the worst.

Fighting will take into account factors like your skill, training, strength and speed compared to that of your opponent, as well as the number of opponents, the environmental conditions at the time and differences in weapons involved on both sides. It will factor in your situational awareness, your ability to react quickly and properly, even your ability to deliver violence with decisive, unforgiving effectiveness. A fight is the most feral, fundamental contest between two human beings.

The Goal of Self-Defense

You should have a goal for any endeavor, and fighting is no exception. Our courtrooms, however, have made the articulation of intent in a fight a critical matter. It is easy, especially in the heat after battle, to speak in anger or fear. Phrases like "shoot to kill" or "I killed that @#&%$!!" fall easily from agitated lips, especially when we just had to fight for our lives. Tragically, those are the kinds of comments that get victims thrown into jail or buried in civil litigation. If there is only one lesson about fighting you take from this book it is this:

In the face of violence, we fight back to stop the attack. Period.

The end state of an assailant, be that living or dead, is most likely beyond your ability to dictate. **We do not shoot or hit "to kill" -- we use whatever tool we have on hand to stop the threat as abruptly as possible.** For very, very serious reasons police refer to this goal as "instant de-animation" [65] and it has tremendous legal implications for officers and citizens alike. With this firmly in mind, we proceed to the chapter on Physical Combat.

---

65   De-Animation simply means to render someone incapable of moving. This does not seek to induce any specific medical condition such as death or coma; it seeks simply to shut down the ability of an attacker to keep attacking. *This can be an absolutely critical legal distinction and articulating anything else can expose you to the worst of legal hazards.*

PHYSICAL COMBAT

"Never start a fight, son, but never fail to finish one."
~Daniel Marks

My father, quoted above, was a U.S. Marine hand-to-hand combat instructor before settling into the much quieter life of an aerospace engineer. As a holdover of his younger days, he gave me a very simple set of rules that went hand-in-hand with the words of John Wayne: "I won't be wronged. I won't be insulted. I won't be laid a-hand on. I don't do these things to other people, and I require the same from them."

At the risk of uttering the dreaded words 'back in my day,' one did not go pick fights with a neighbor. I was expected even as a boy to conduct myself as a gentleman. But I was taught at a very young age that not everybody played by the same set of rules and that some people, even school-aged kids, took great delight in making the lives of weaker people an utter living misery. I could not have imagined in my comparatively innocent youth the kinds of abuse dished out by bullies today. But the lesson my father taught me then remains as essential now as it did those many years ago. If you fail to finish a fight, the other guy will finish it for you.

This book was not written to be a how-to manual for physical combat. How you fight -- be that driven by choice or by necessity -- is an immensely personalized matter that should suit your physiology, age, speed and size among numerous other attributes. It should take into consideration some socially unpleasant things like your capacity for violence.[66] There are numerous ways to approach a fight and while the proponents of any one style may loudly crow that it is better than another, what is important is what works for you. The spinning, leaping art of Tae-Kwon-Do may be an awesome choice for the young and agile but may be less suited for those of us who are at a point of being a bit more, well, gravitationally challenged.

> **If you are seriously interested in learning to fight you should enroll in a class offered by a reputable school or instructor, in a style suited to your capabilities.**

Learning any physical skill from tennis to fencing requires practice to develop the body mechanics needed to perform at your best. Martial arts of any kind, from unarmed to armed combat, can be huge fun and provide a tremendous source of exercise, focus and accomplishment. In my experience I have found the people I have met in these venues to be largely outgoing and energetic and very generous with their knowledge and time. Many schools offer an introductory chance to participate in or, at the very least, to watch a class with no commitment.

---

66 That may sound rather dark but consider what a mom would do to protect her kids. Capacity for violence is separate and distinct from a desire to inflict harm. Some people truly are incapable of violence, even in the face of certain death, and die like sheep. Fighters, even those forced to fight, must have a mental and physical capacity to inflict grievous injury without hesitation if they are to prevail in a serious fight.

If you find that a hard-style martial art (think punching and kicking) is not to your liking, the grab-and-shove aspects of a soft-style might be a better fit. Those interested in shooting may be put off by the focus of a defensive sport but fall in love with the precision of target shooting. The important part is finding ways to develop real-world hands-on skills. Whatever your interest, nothing will provide you with a greater degree of knowledge and familiarity than getting getting involved in qualified instructor-led training.

That said, we can examine a few introductory aspects of human physiology and fight mechanics suitable to be presented in this forum. These are offered to establish a very preliminary baseline of combat-related terms that can serve you in your search for more comprehensive training in a martial art. To be clear, this introduction is limited in focus to self-defense, not sports. The information presented here is selected and organized with respect to the ability to disable an opponent as abruptly as possible. It is not a nice idea, but as you have already read, neither is being assaulted.

In the case of straightforward assault, as opposed to robbery for example, a Bad Guy's goal is to hurt you. To stop that, the logical course of action is to inflict debilitating harm on him before you get hurt. Going into a fight the Bad Guy will look at you like a butcher looks at a piece of meat; deciding what part of you looks to be the most vulnerable. Whether it is to protect those places on your own body or to exploit the same vulnerabilities on your assailant, you should have a basic grasp of physiology.

Humans come in a myriad of different shapes and sizes, from scrawny and brittle to massive and muscle-clad. Morbid obesity might look like a weakness but, while ruining mobility, a thick layer of flab can act like bubble-wrap to protect vital organs inside.

As this is an introductory study, we will limit our focus on the primary areas of vulnerability with an important caveat: **differences in physical size and muscle mass may limit or exaggerate the vulnerability of target areas in any given fight.** That said, let's take a very brief look at a bit of human anatomy.

The Brain

The brain is a little under 3lbs of spongy tissue that drives everything. It is the top of our central nervous system (CNS) that controls every muscle in our body. If the brain stops, everything stops. Personal strength and determination cease to matter if the brain is destroyed or disconnected from the rest of the body.

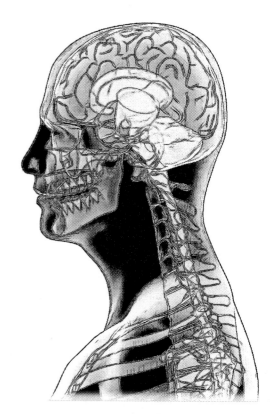

Since the soft, spongy brain is so vital to life, nature gave us a skull to act as a crash helmet. But a skull has limits; a high-energy weapon like a gun, hammer, crowbar or baseball bat can deliver enough force to bash through that armor. As we see in car wrecks and sports injuries, a violent impact or twist to the head or neck may damage the spinal cord, cutting communication between the brain and the rest of the body. This can result in various medical conditions ranging from disability or unconsciousness to paralysis and death.

Traumatic injury to the CNS is more likely than any other attack to de-animate or debilitate a violent threat.

The Eyes

Eyes are very sensitive and the eyeballs of the most muscled-up Bad Guy are no tougher than yours. Anything you can violently jammed into an eye, from fingers or ballpoint pen to a steak knife or screwdriver, can cause intense pain and instantly diminish an attacker's ability to see. While not as definitive as taking away a Bad Guy's ability to move, depriving him of sight can be a real tactical advantage.

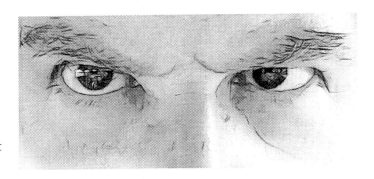

An eye is held in the socket by muscles that act much like rubber bands. A finger, thumb or object driven forcefully into an eye socket can displace the eye right out of the skull. Now that may sound really icky, but there is a good chance that a Bad Guy won't want to fight after you've popped an eyeball out of his head.

The back of the eye socket itself is much thinner than the rest of the skull and a long object driven into the eye with sufficient force may penetrate into the brain.

Beyond brute force attack, the eyes are very sensitive to abrasion or corrosives. A fistful of sand, dirt or most any household chemical like bleach can play havoc with an assailant's vision. Although an obvious fire hazard, gasoline in the eyes can be terribly painful and damaging to vision.

While injury to the eye is less likely to prove de-animating, depriving a Bad Guy of sight may reduce his ability to hurt you and can open numerous options for escaping or finishing the fight.

The Nose

There is a longstanding myth that a sharp upward blow into the base of the nose can drive shards of cartilage into the brain with sudden lethal effect. Chuck Norris might pull it off but this tactic has low odds for mere mortals.

That does not eliminate the middle of the face as a target; the nose is a sensitive region and a solid blow can be blindingly painful, potentially causing the eyes to water and obscure vision. The face is very vascular and a busted nose can bleed profusely. A truly severe blow may crush the nostrils and obstruct an opponent's ability to breathe easily; this is not likely an instantly disabling injury but can reduce an opponents stamina to fight or chase you. A damaged sinus can bleed profusely, draining down the throat and into the lungs. The nose is particularly susceptible to solid blunt weapons that offer superior impact and crushing force. A brick across the nose will likely have far greater debilitating effect than a similar blow on a large, fleshy muscle.

The Windpipe

The windpipe is basically a tube of cartilage that runs down the center front of the throat. It is the passage through which we breathe and it is tough, but breakable. A solid blow, especially with a hard weapon, can damage that tube or send it into spasm. The respiratory factors noted regarding the nose apply to the windpipe as well.

The Pelvis

The pelvis is a wide, vaguely butterfly-shaped piece of bone that serves as the anchor point for our legs. If the pelvis breaks, the legs may cease to function properly. While a Bad Guy on the ground may still be able to hurt you, taking away his ability to walk can greatly enhance your ability to get out of reach.

By design the pelvis is tough and a great deal of impact force is required to break one. Few of us will likely have a sledgehammer on hand for a fight so in all general likelihood only a gun will provide pelvis-breaking force. Police train to shoot at the pelvis as a means of stopping the advance of a hostile aggressor, notably ones that do not seem to react to other types of force.

Bleeding

Cut anybody and they will bleed, but some areas bleed more than others. Humans on average have about six pints of blood in their bodies. A loss of two pints is considered a serious hazard while losing four pints or more can be fatal.

It is an easy analogy to think about the human circulatory system like a roadway that carries blood through a city. If you have a wreck on a narrow country road the effects will be minor, but a crash on a four-lane highway can result in a hundred-car pile-up.[67] In terms of a fight, the important four-lane highways of the circulatory system include the vessels of the heart (such as the Aorta, Pulmonary Artery and Vena Cava), the Femoral Artery, the Carotid Artery and Jugular Vein, the Subclavian Artery, the Radial Artery and the Renal and Hepatic Arteries. Opening one or more of these vessels can result in rapid blood loss. This can produce a condition known as hypovolemia and ultimately death. You desperately want to avoid having this happen to you and protecting these vulnerable areas is an important consideration.

Inducing bleeding of any sort may have a tactical value in a fight. Some people lack the stomach for blood, especially their own, and may panic at the sight. Even if they persist, a severe cut inflicted on a Bad Guy will likely continue to bleed without further effort on your part. New options for you to finish or flee the fight may arise as the Bad Guy's condition deteriorates, or while he struggles to stop the bleeding.

Blood-Borne Pathogens

Keep in mind that blood carries disease and contact with a stranger's blood, especially that of a violent criminal, comes with a risk. To the extent possible you should try to avoid contact with a Bad Guy's blood and certainly keep it out of your eyes, mouth or any open wounds on your body. While it is imperative to survive a fight, it is just as important to avoid a life-changing contamination.

If you are defending yourself from an edged weapon it is critical to protect your inner forearms. You may choose to wrap an arm for blocking. If you get cut, especially if you see blood pulsing from a wound, as quickly as possible apply firm direct pressure above the wound[68]. Many items from a piece of cord to a belt or strip of fabric can be used to help maintain this pressure until help arrives.

---

67   This is no exaggeration. See events like http://www.youtube.com/watch?v=kC2y3b86AOA

68   Above the wound does not refer to height, but to the proximity to the heart. The farther from the heart, the "lower" the wound. Thus if cut on the wrist, direct pressure could be applied to the forearm to reduce the bleeding.

If you have been stabbed and the weapon is stuck in you,[69] do not pull it out as this can worsen the bleeding and inflict additional damage. Make every effort not to move the embedded weapon and call for immediate medical attention.

Vital Organs

Beyond those already mentioned, human bodies have a few other parts that can be critical in a fight.

Damage to the heart can prove rapidly de-animating but, much like the skull exists to protect the brain, we have a ribcage and sternum which protects the heart. The sternum is a slab of bone that acts like an armor plate over the heart, held in place by a cage of bones that wrap around many of our vital organs. The ribcage is amazingly resilient and can absorb huge impact forces like those dished out in a car wreck.

The ribcage itself is further wrapped in layers of muscle and fat which, in the case of a beefy opponent, can be thick and tough. While there have been many instances when a heart has been punctured with a knife or other sharp object, such events hinge as much on luck, be it good or bad, on the part of the recipient. Barring cases of extreme body mass, defensive ammunition commonly employed by police, such as 9mm or .45ACP, has demonstrated the ability to punch through a chest wall and into the organs beyond.

Injury to the lungs can prove critical but not necessarily immediate. Some people have not only survived in the wake of a severe lung injury but have continued to function for an extended period.

The liver and kidneys are sensitive to impact and highly vascular; a puncture in either of these organs can produce excruciating pain and rapid bleeding.

TACTICAL FUNDAMENTALS

As mentioned earlier, there is no substitute for professional, in-person training when it comes to fighting. Even if you have no desire to fight, if you cannot imagine the need for physical combat, you would be well served to take at least an introductory self-defense course from a reputable instructor. A basic lesson on simple fight mechanics can greatly enhance your capabilities should you decide, in the darkest of moments, that you need them.

There is a military axiom that says "In a crisis we do not rise to our expectations, we fall back to our training." That means you will likely perform only as well as you have trained and practiced. There are, however, a few very fundamental concepts of fighting that you may wish to consider prior to any subsequent training.

Unless you are in a barren setting like an empty parking lot, the environment around you may offer a number of improvised weapons, especially at home or work. Common items like scissors, a steak knife, a fire extinguisher or any other solid object can be useful in a fight.

The human hand is made up of small bones. If you slam a ball of small bones (your fist) against a large tough bone (like somebody's skull) it is more likely that the hand will break than the skull. Boxers wear gloves for a reason.

Compared to fists, elbows and knees can deliver significant impact with less risk of injury to yourself. An elbow is capable of striking forward as well as backward, which can be particularly useful in confined spaces like an elevator or when grappling. Elbows and knees more directly employ larger muscles and the rotation of your torso to add strength.

---

69   This is a common occurrence - example http://www.theage.com.au/victoria/man-found-with-knife-blade-in-neck-after-fight-20100223-os8i.html

Feet are made up of small bones much like the hand, but most of us go through life wearing shoes that protect our feet and allow us to kick with greater force and less risk of self-injury. Boots, especially heavy ones like steel-toed work boots, can increase your potential impact force considerably. While high-heel shoes are a hindrance to running, they can be a deadly asset if brought down (in a stomping motion) onto the top of an opponent's foot or into the body. A high-heel shoe in hand, struck spike-first, can also serve as a credible makeshift weapon.[70]

On the subject of weapons in general, almost any solid object has the potential of being useful in a fight. If it has a point or sharp edge it may be able to inflict a cut or puncture better than your bare hands. If it is solid and has weight it may strike harder than a fist. If you find yourself being threatened, you should start looking for routes of escape and any tools that can be used to improve your ability to fight.

Defensively, protect your vulnerable spots. Boxers keep their arms raised to protect their heads; if professionals do it, common sense suggests that it is a good idea. The outside of your forearm is typically less vulnerable than the soft inside where larger blood vessels can be more easily cut. Keeping your hands up, your palms facing you, reduces the amount of vulnerable area directly exposed to attack.

To be explicitly clear - fighting is not an option to be taken lightly. It is not macho or glorious, nor is it a preferrable first choice for reasons that span injury, infection, litigation and prosecution. If this chapter does nothing else it should reinforce your proactive interest in Feign, Fortress and Flight as prior alternatives. Every second that a fight continues increases your risk of a bad outcome.

That said, there are times when fighting is all you have, and in those moments you should fight with unflinching ferocity. To support that contention I offer the wisdom of legendary General George Patton Jr. who said:

> **"There is only one tactical principle which is not subject to change.**
> **It is to use the means at hand to inflict the maximum amount of wound,**
> **death, and destruction on the enemy in the minimum amount of time."**

That is an ugly thought, but fighting is ugly. If you decide to strike, do so with all of the force you can muster. Strike with the intent not to touch the front surface of your target, but to drive your blow out through the back. Once you start, keep hitting it until it cannot hit back. And even if the fight appears to be over, do not relinquish or drop whatever weapon you may have in hand, lest you be caught without it or worse yet, that it fall into the hands of your opponent.[71]

---

70   This is no exaggeration. In 2013 Houston resident Ana Lilia Trujillo told police she was being attacked by Alf Andersson when she stabbed him to death with her stiletto high heels. http://www.youtube.com/watch?v=kU8PF3tnePc

71   The one caveat to this last point pertains to the moment that police arrive on the scene. You do not want to point a weapon of any sort at an officer, nor behave in a belligerent or threatening manner. If you have just been in a high-stress event your nerves will be on edge and your judgement strained; this is a time to follow the directions of police immediately.

In Summary:

If you have ever watched a movie scene set in a casino, you doubtlessly have seen some character place the huge all-or-nothing bet. "Let it all ride on red!" While there is arguably some slim chance for a big payoff, most people in the audience know this is the point where the foolhardy gambler gets cleaned out.

An intelligent strategy for anything, be it gambling, business, investments or personal safety, is to diversify. By leveraging the best parts of different strategies and picking the ones that work for you, you can most effectively manage aspects of the Four Fs in ways that are most comfortable.

There is no perfect solution, no one-size-fits-all plan. Steps that are critical to one person might be a meaningless expense for another. As we said in the beginning, spending time, effort or money on something that does not make your life better is a waste, and takes away from things that might pay you a better return.

For the best results, choose the tools and tactics that favor your abilities. One might consider the words of Damon Runyon when he said, "The race is not always to the swift nor the battle to the strong, but that's certainly the way to bet."

So let's get down to the nitty-gritty and look at some of the actual tools and tactics that you can employ in your defense. We will cover the strengths, weaknesses and hazards to help you make an informed decision.

70

THE ART OF WAR

"For to win one hundred victories on one hundred battles is not the acme of skill.
To subdue the enemy without fighting is the acme of skill"
~ Sun Tzu

And thus we come to the point where the rubber meets the road and all academic thought gives way to specific plans and measures. The ideal goal, as we have established, is not to win fights but to avoid them. However, if we are forced to fight, we must exploit every resource, technique and tactic at our disposal to end the fight quickly and make sure that in the very least, our herd is the one that survives.

Our explorations into the tactical world begin with a few simple rules that summarize elements presented thus far.

RULE 1: YOU CAN'T AVOID WHAT YOU DO NOT SEE
You cannot make an intelligent decision about a threat of which you are unaware. The first and most essential step in any safety plan is simply to keep your eyes and ears open to the world around you. This provides two benefits at the same time. First, of course, is a heightened situational awareness and the ability to detect threats or avoid dangerous environments. The second is that our being aware changes our outward appearance. Criminals like the element of surprise and look for targets who will not see them coming. If you walk down the street with your head up, eyes scanning your surroundings, you appear less vulnerable. If you do nothing else to begin your safety efforts... pay attention.

RULE 2: DISTANCE IS YOUR FRIEND
There are few hard and fast rules you can apply across the range of possible emergencies, but one you can count on is that you cannot make your situation worse by intelligently moving away from a threat.[72] If you can maintain even a few feet of separation from an assailant you can make physical contact difficult or even impossible.[73] With every additional yard of separation you become statistically more difficult to hit with thrown objects, bullets or other missiles. Even explosive force diminishes with distance and fragments slow down as they travel. Anything you do to separate yourself from a perceived threat will reduce its ability to reach out and touch you.

---

72   In saying "intelligently" we are excluding the notion of making a tunnel-vision dash away from one threat and running blindly into another. In a grim internet video (which will not be cited due to the graphic nature of the website upon which it was displayed) a boy walking down the street was startled by an aggressive dog; the boy looked back at the dog as he ran into the street, unwittingly into the path of a bus.

73   The precise distance dependent on the length of their arms or the stick they may be carrying at the moment but the point being, even a little distance can put you out of reach.

RULE 3: INTERVENING BARRIERS ARE YOUR FRIENDS TOO

Next to distance, putting anything solid between yourself and a threat makes it harder for the harmful force to reach you. Most physical threat is measured in terms of force. Every time an attack has to punch through an intervening barrier it loses force, often a great deal of force. A sufficient barrier, or series of barriers, can stop an attack altogether.

This is a simple concept that has been portrayed on almost every TV gunfight you have ever seen; combatants trade shots while intermittently ducking behind some solid object. Bullets that were otherwise on the mark bury into, or ricochet off of, whatever barrier is in use.

Consider this in contrast to an equally common Hollywood example of poor decision-making shown when some Good Guy on foot is being pursued by a Bad Guy in a car. The victim invariably runs down the centerline of the road where the car overtakes and flattens him. Had our victim zig-zagged between every parked car and tree, the vehicle would have lost all ability to make contact.

One of the most astounding examples of this strategy was captured on video on Feb 24, 2006. A man approached a lawyer outside a Van Nuys, CA courthouse and began to fire at him with a handgun. Having no place better to hide, the lawyer stepped behind a tree for cover. Although the two figures were close enough to touch one another, the lawyer was able to shift left and right behind the tree and avoid being hit although several shots were fired. The assailant finally ran out of bullets and simply walked away. As absurd as it seems, the tree provided enough visual and physical barrier to keep the victim safe.[74]

Entering a solidly constructed building or moving around any sizeable object that breaks your line-of-sight with a hazard can provide some degree of physical barrier against a threat that is on the other side.[75]

RULE 4: DUTY TO WARN

Civilians have no duty to issue any type of warning to somebody who is attacking them. That's right, none. The antiquated notion of a fair fight seems civilized and honorable but there is no basis for it in modern law.[76] Your decision to use force should be predicated on your ability to articulate afterwards why you felt you were in danger and, in some jurisdictions, to explain that you had exhausted reasonable measures to get away or mitigate the threat.

Presuming a clearly evident threat (such as a Bad Guy entering your bedroom with a machete in hand) you are under no obligation to express your defensive intent or give the Bad Guy a chance to repent of his evil ways. In fact doing so may in some circumstances place you at even greater risk. The element of surprise can be a powerful advantage in any conflict and could spell the difference in the outcome of a fight.

Most specifically and emphatically, you should never, ever fire a "warning shot" of any sort with a firearm. Doing so will likely place you at grave risk for severe criminal charges and civil liabilities levied against you.

---

74   http://www.youtube.com/watch?v=H9zy37-_0LU

75   There are limits to the amount of force that any object can absorb or defeat. That is a "why" question that involves terms like mass, weight and velocity. In simple analogy, a truck may protect you from the effects of a small explosion while a rather large blast might hurl or shred the entire truck. In general, the bigger the barrier, the better. A Volkswagen would provide more protection than a bicycle, while a concrete building is better yet.

76   While intended as comedy, fictional character Jayne Cobb in the TV series Firefly said "Hell I'll kill a man in a fair fight... or if I think he's gonna start a fair fight." The underlying point is that nobody on this planet has a right to hurt you. The term "Fair Fight" is a contrivance for sports like boxing. In real life there is getting hurt or killed and not getting hurt; should somebody attack you it is by definition "unfair" and you should use any tactic or tool at your disposal to minimize the injury the attacker is trying to inflict upon you.

RULE 5: DUTY TO RENDER AID

Most of us grew up in a world where we feel obliged to assist the injured. It is not in our nature to stand by while somebody screams for help. However, much like the Duty to Warn, there is no specific duty to render aid to somebody who presented a danger to you - either by threatening you or actually attacking you.

Someone who has been injured as a direct or indirect result of a criminal act of violence should be considered dangerous until secured by the police. Do not approach, do not attempt to get a better look at their injuries, do not let yourself get sucked in by pleas for help.[77]

The logic is simple: you never, ever want to be close to a violent person - be they chasing you or flat on the ground and screaming. Even injured people can lash out in anger, in drug-fueled insanity or by using the appearance of injury as a ruse to draw you into range. As noted earlier, the injured person may be bleeding, and contact with their blood or other body fluids can put you at risk for blood-borne pathogens. Stay away.

There is no scenario in which your safety improves by moving closer to a violent Bad Guy, regardless of his condition. The moment an assailant is no longer able to hurt or pursue you, be it a brief moment or for what appears to be a permanent disability, get away to a safe location as fast as you can and call 911.[78]

Never assume that the risk from an injured Bad Guy is over or diminished, even if the injury he suffered appears catastrophic. Continue to act as though the threat remains clear and present until police officers arrive and secure the scene.

RULE 6. THE DUTY TO COMPLY WITH POLICE

This is a point that is often overlooked but one that has tremendous implications. Officers arriving on the scene will not have some magical advance knowledge of your situation. There is no guarantee that things told to a 911 operator will make it to the officers en route. An officer may find you face down and injured, or find you standing while an injured assailant lies on the ground. When first confronted with the scene, the officer may have no idea which one of you is the criminal and which is the victim.[79]

Keep in mind, at this moment the officer will have the same concern for his own safety as he does for yours. The officer will immediately begin to issue instructions, likely to show your hands to be empty, or to get down on the ground. This is not some power play or game. **You have a legal duty to comply with a police officer's instructions; failure to do so places you, as well as the officer, at a greater risk of harm.**

In a complex or dynamic situation an officer may go as far as to handcuff people or secure them inside a vehicle. These actions carry no expressions of presumed guilt or innocence; they are merely a means of getting control of a dangerous situation. The officer's first priority is to ensure that nobody else gets hurt; separating the players is one way to keep them from hurting one another.

---

77 The notion of Feign mentioned earlier is commonly used by Bad Guys to lure victims into reach. They may do so to strip you of the range advantage of a weapon you might have, or merely to get close enough to surprise you with a sudden violent action.

78 In the course of assessing the situation, a 911 operator may ask questions like "is he breathing?" or "how badly is he hurt?" Odds are you are not a doctor, paramedic or coroner so the simple answer is "I don't know and I'm not getting near enough to find out." If you have locked yourself in a secure room, you take a risk if you open the door to take a peek.

79 In fact, it is a good idea to raise your hands and shout "VICTIM!" as an officer first approaches. While they are not likely to take anything at face value, this can help to establish identity in those first few seconds. In the very least, it is a non-hostile act.

If police arrive during or after a violent incident, follow the officer's directions promptly and without argument. If you distract the officer with your own behavior you may provide the real criminal with an opening to attack or to escape.

This transition phase can be a challenging one. The threat posed by a criminal does not cease the moment an officer pulls up on the scene. A Bad Guy may panic on seeing police arrive and may continue to inflict harm until properly secured, which normally means in handcuffs and locked in a vehicle or otherwise restrained.

You may have a weapon in hand that you have used to keep a threat at bay and simply dropping that weapon when the police first arrive may place it where a Bad Guy can get it. That puts everybody at risk. But this highlights an EXTREMELY important point: You need to be mindful that you have a weapon in your hand - be it a gun, brick, baseball bat or anything else.

NEVER EVER point a weapon of ANY type in the direction of police.

An officer may reasonably perceive that as a threat and respond in a way that turns out very badly for everybody involved. **Immediately** following police instructions in this case is more critical than ever.

Whether you are armed or not, you should make an immediate gesture of submission towards responding officers, like raising one or both hands, fingers open, to let them know you are not a threat. You may be amped up on adrenaline and fear, you may be hurt, but this is not the moment to try to blurt out your story. You will have ample opportunity once the scene is secure. This is a time to listen carefully and follow directions. It may sound like a cliché but the only answer that should come out of your mouth is "Yes Sir" because that, more than anything else, will convey a non-threatening, law-abiding attitude.[80]

RULE 7. DUTY TO BE RIGHT

At the end of all things, you owe it to yourself to be right. That may sound strange, but anybody who has read a newspaper or watched a news program in the last twenty years can tell you that good intention and common sense may mean nothing in the wake of a violent encounter.

Many people, police officers included, have ended up in life-altering trouble after taking action against an aggressor who appeared to be armed with a deadly weapon that later proved to be a cellphone, a toy, or other inert object. What may seem to you like a terrifying split-second, live-or-die moment will almost certainly be picked apart by lawyers one thread at a time in an effort to convince a jury that whatever decision you made was wrong.

"How did you know the criminal would hurt you...?" they will ask. "How could you be certain...?"

This is a disingenuous standard. Humans lack the ability to predict the future. We count on certain things like gravity to be reasonably constant, but we will never know, in the God-like omniscient sense, what another human being will do in the next moment. We react to what we believe based on the evidence in front of us, and will never know anything until it has already happened.

---

80   And maybe just keep in mind that the officer giving you those directions just came racing here to stand between you and danger when he was safely somewhere else to begin with. A little bit of appreciation really does go a long way.

This brings us to a point of separating emotion and tradition from our analysis. I know people who say they would wreak bloody havoc "if somebody ever... threatened my kids, broke into my house, etc." Like most people I understand that sentiment and recognize the tendency we have to draw our lines in the sand. In an earlier America that was a more legally survivable proposition.

But in today's America, no matter how things appeared at the time of a criminal attack, an average citizen may well be crucified after the facts have been studied for days, weeks or even months. What if the gun in the Bad Guy's hand turned out to be a realistic airsoft toy?[81] What if the face under the mask is later revealed to be a different color of skin than yours and someone asserts your actions were motivated by race? People who acted in honest fear for their safety have gone on to see their lives, homes and fortunes flushed away on just such turns of fact.

So what does this mean?

Clearly you do not want to accept a risk to life and limb for fear of wrongful litigation. There is an old axiom that says, "I would rather be judged by twelve than carried by six." But the reality of today's America raises the ante for how and where you draw your line in the sand in terms of a defensive action. If you are not entirely clear as to the nature of a threat and you feel you have sufficient intervening barrier, you could be better-served to make any attempt to further clarify the situation before you take action.

Consider a home invasion scenario: although it may seem improbable at the moment, somebody might have entered your house by a sincere or drunken mistake, or to seek aid in a crisis of their own.[82] This risk highlights another benefit of the Fortify strategy in providing you with the means to clarify or safely extend a situation that might otherwise be unclear.

You have a duty to yourself to be found legally right when the smoke clears, and you will likely never have all the facts up front. This means you need to stay calm and think in a crisis, you need to be able to articulate why you took the action you did and possibly why you did not avail yourself of alternatives. Think clearly, act rationally and be ready to give a good reason for the choices you make.

REACTION GAP

When you hear a phrase like "the speed of thought" it is easy to take that to mean "instantly." You may be surprised to know that quite the opposite is true. It takes time for the light that strikes your eye to be processed into a visual picture that your brain can even start to consider. Not a lot of time, mind you, but on average it takes most people at least three-quarters of a second for the brain to react to an outside stimulus. In combative training this is called the Reaction Gap.

That may not seem like much time at all, but a lot can happen in just a second. When you add stress or unexpected events, that gap can stretch on for several seconds. You have doubtlessly seen real events or news footage where a frightening event occurs and some people just stand shock-frozen in place. These are people in a stuck Reaction Gap, brains unable to process events and provide even reflex-level direction.

---

81   Which of course is why some Bad Guys have committed crimes with toy guns, having no real one to use, in hopes that the average citizen will not be able to tell the difference and comply through fear of what looks to be a real weapon.

82   See the case study of Zoey Ripple presented later in this book.

If you are talking, your Reaction Gap is typically greater than if you are quiet and paying attention. On rare occasions, Hollywood has presented this accurately. In the Tom Cruise flick *Collateral*, assassin Vincent encounters a pair common thugs, one with gun in hand, having just robbed another character. Vincent poses a question: "Is that my briefcase?" The thug with the gun begin to speak and Vincent responds with sudden, unexpected swiftness. The fight was over before either thug recognized that it had begun. Admittedly this is a fictional example but, with training, one can draw and put two rounds into an up-close target in less than a second.

Reaction Gap may be a fleeting moment, but it can be time enough for one sudden, definitive act that changes the tide of battle. It may allow you to shoot or strike or to break contact and get away. If you choose to exploit this vulnerability, make sure your action is emphatic.

With Reaction Gap in mind, should you find yourself in a stressful, high-threat scenario... shut up. That might sound harsh but this is not the time for idle conversation or venting emotion, it is a time for watching and thinking. If you must speak, keep your statements short and direct. If you have made the decision to act in a way that might benefit from a brief head start, getting your opponent to talk or visually track a brief distraction may help that equation to some degree.

MAKING A GOOD 911 CALL

As discussed earlier, calling 911 is likely the first and most essential step to soliciting help in your time of need. When you call 911, for yourself or somebody else, you will be under great stress, possibly having one of the worst days of your life. In great stress, we are rarely at our best. Understanding how 911 works and how to get the best of the system will improve the speed and quality of your response.

The 911 system runs on a process and you want it to run as fast as possible. This is not the time to argue or try to run the conversation. 911 operators need to know certain things and the best thing you can do for yourself is to listen to their questions and answer them clearly and succinctly. Above all - do your best to stay calm. Time you spend crying, screaming or babbling is only adding time that must pass before help arrives.

The most important two questions the 911 operator will ask you is where you are and what is the nature of your emergency. If you are calling from a land-line it is likely that the phone company computer will pinpoint your location automatically, but that is not guaranteed. If you are calling from a cell phone, the phone system may not know where you are standing. When initially asked where you are, operators are NOT looking for answers like "in the driveway" or "at my grandmother's house." Those may be true, but not very helpful. You should always start with the name of the city and state[83] you are in, or if you are in a rural area start with a reference to the closest city.

"I am in Gainesville, Florida." or...

"I am on route 50 about three miles west of Gainesville, Florida."

If you are at a location that may be recognizable or clearly marked, it may help responders if you provide that additional information.

"I am at the Burger King on Route 50 about three miles west of Gainesville, FL."

---

83   State is important as the 911 system is widespread and there may be a dozen towns with the same name as yours across the country. The answer "Miami" may put you in Florida or Ohio.

As to the nature of your emergency, be SUCCINCT. Your story does not begin with "Well we went out to the library and decided to get a burger..." The 911 operator's fingers are poised over buttons that say POLICE, FIRE and EMS and they need the immediate details to know which ones to push. Clear, specific answers are more likely to give the 911 operator an accurate picture and trigger the best responses:

"My dad is on the ground clutching his chest."
- 911 dispatches EMS

"Somebody is breaking into my house."
- 911 dispatches Police on high alert and have EMS on standby

"There has been a terrible pile-up on the highway, cars are on fire and people are hurt badly."
- 911 dispatches everybody.

At points during the call you may hear a series of clicks. If so, DO NOT hang up! Your call may be routed to the closest 911 call center that is most familiar with your area and has the most immediate control of response assets close to you. Stay calm; if you have done a clear job answering the first two questions, help is already on the way.

The 911 operator may ask you follow-up questions. Keep in mind that while you may be aware of everything around you, operators know only what you tell them. You are their eyes and ears and in asking you questions, they are in essence trying to "look at the situation" to get you the best help.

While you may not be a trained medical professional and your stress reaction might be "how the hell do I know?" the reality is that if you focus on details, you can likely provide information valuable to a response effort.

Is the victim breathing?
Do you see the chest rise and fall? If it is cold do you see the fog of breath? If there is blood in mouth or nose, do you see bubbles forming rhythmically? These phenomena all suggest that the victim is breathing.

Does the victim have a pulse?
If you gently place your fingers on the chest, along the side of the throat, or on the inside of the wrist, you should be able to feel a heartbeat. It may feel different at each location. It is a good idea to try this when people are healthy so you can get an idea what a normal pulse feels like.

Is the victim conscious?
Is one or both eyes open and looking around? Does the victim respond to spoken words or a sharp sound like a finger snap or clap? If someone is reacting to the world around them, they are to some degree conscious.

Responders will seek information that goes beyond the condition of a victim. Before charging into your crisis, responders understandably want to know if a threat is still active in the area. If you have reported a situation where you are in danger from someone around you, like a burglar in the house for example, operators will typically ask yes-or-no questions that you can answer quietly if you are in hiding.

If you think it is frustrating having to answer these questions in a crisis, imagine how frustrating it must be trying to save the life of somebody who will not provide the information needed to do so.

Nobody has more to lose in an emergency than the person calling 911, so it is in your best interest to pull it together. Listen carefully to the operator's questions; while some may strike you as redundant to something you have already answered, the question may be trying to reveal additional specifics that can help the response, or to clarify the risk to police and response personnel. In the case of a criminal attack, for example, it does you no good if the responding officer is killed coming in the door because he did not know that an armed assailant was still inside. Let the operator guide the conversation and keep your answers short and direct.

During a 911 emergency you may be directed by the operator to take certain actions. These instructions should guide you to improving the situation while help is on the way. The operator may advise you to make some sort of medical intervention, like applying a tourniquet or performing CPR, or may instruct you to get farther away from the danger.

This does raise another "what" question: what do you do if the 911 operator tells you to render aid to your assailant, and act which may place you at greater danger? The short answer is you should always do what you believe provides you with the greatest measure of safety. Beyond that however, in many if not most jurisdictions 911 operators are dispatchers, not sworn officers. As such, they would not carry the same legal authority. This is a good point to check in your location and a call to your local police department will clarify the law in your area.

Keep your eyes and ears open throughout the call. It may be helpful to the operator to know when you hear an approaching siren or helicopter, or when conditions on the scene change. The delayed onset of fire, for example, might be a critical factor requiring the dispatch of additional units, while the departure of violent criminals from the scene might require additional police to pursue and capture.

Details can be important, especially details that pertain to visual identification. The number of people involved and the color of clothing are two very easy observations, as well as the color and type of vehicles that might be involved. While many people do not know anything about makes and models of cars or guns, almost anybody can note details such as "two guys drove off in a beat-up green pickup truck. The guy in the blue hoodie had a silver handgun."

Do not hang up until instructed to do so by the 911 operator. If for any reason you run into a recorded message, listen to it and follow instructions. If you are disconnected, re-dial 911.

As a reminder:
If you are calling for help in the process or aftermath of a criminal encounter, keep in mind that the officers coming to your aid have a reasonable concern for their own safety, especially if the Bad Guy is still in the area. It may be helpful to give the 911 operator your most obvious visual description so that police can distinguish you (who they have never seen before) from anybody else on the scene. When officers arrive do not run towards them and under no circumstance whatsoever should you approach a responding officer with a weapon in your hands. Standing still with your hands raised in plain view is the quickest way to show an officer that you are not a threat. If an officer issues a command, you should comply. This isn't personal; the officer is just trying to get control of a completely unfamiliar situation that may place other lives in jeopardy as well as yours.

Also keep in mind that 911 calls are recorded. All of them. So everything you say in the heat of fear or anger can come back weeks, months or even years later to haunt you in a court of law. The 911 system is there to provide you with life-critical support, not to document your story or hear your confession, so take a page from the old TV show *Dragnet* and stick with "the facts, just the facts."

Case Study: Josephone County, OR 911

Of course, not all things work the way they should. The 911 system is as susceptible as any other human enterprise to budget cuts and the occasional dim-witted employee. This was glaringly highlighted in 2012 when an Oregon woman called 911 to report that Michael Bellah was again breaking into her home. The last time he had done so Bellah had sexually assaulted the woman, leaving her hospitalized for weeks. Despite the grave threat, the 911 operator stated "Uh, I don't have anybody to send out there. You know, obviously, if he comes inside the residence and assaults you, can you ask him to go away?"[84] Imagine yourself in that situation for just a moment and you can decide for yourself that you need to make provisions for your own defense.

It is impossible to predict and train for every possible combination of facts. Instead, we will look at different types of scenarios and consider the potential risks and rewards of available options. These scenarios are based on some of the disturbing events in recent news that may be unfamiliar to the average citizen. They have been selected as each representing a different set of dynamics that may require a different set of responses. As you read the initial scenario, ask yourself what you would do in that situation, then read through the possible outcomes that follow.

---

84   http://seattle.cbslocal.com/2013/05/23/911-dispatcher-tells-woman-about-to-be-sexually-assaulted-there-are-no-cops-to-help-her-due-to-budget-cuts/

SCENARIO: THE ABANDONED PACKAGE

The game has been over for twenty minutes but the stadium is still bustling with fans. You stand elbow to elbow with a hundred other people all wearing the same two colors, a sea of matching jerseys and hats highlighted with banners and face paint. The home team just pulled off an amazing win to make it into the playoffs and everybody's spirits are high. A dozen or more revelers off to your left are singing the team fight song, the melody slurred by four quarters of beer consumption. Somebody moving through the crowd pauses to set a backpack on the ground with a dull, heavy thud. It strikes you as odd that someone would lug so heavy a pack to a football game and your eyes flick to the left. The owner of the pack is out of place, clad in a nondescript, dull grey hoodie and a ball cap pulled low over his eyes. He glances around for just a moment, then walks away leaving the pack on the floor. You watch as he disappears into the crowd with what seems like a vague sense of urgency. He does not look back. You look down at the backpack and feel a sense of unease...

Compared to other parts of the world, public bombings are comparatively rare in the United States, although incidents such as the Centennial Olympic Park bombing[85] followed a fact pattern similar to the scenario above. In recent years we have seen attacks of this kind in a train station in Madrid[86] and the London Underground subway.[87] Most recently this scenario played out at the Boston Marathon in an event that provides us with a vivid case study.

Case study: Boston Marathon Bombing 2013
This is the sad story of Jeff Bauman, age 27, who was severely injured at the Boston Marathon Bombing. Waking up at the hospital under heavy sedation Mr. Bauman asked for a pen and wrote "bag, saw the guy, looked right at me." In a news report just after the accident Jeff's brother elaborated that a man wearing a cap, sunglasses and black jacket over a hooded sweatshirt looked at Jeff and dropped a bag at his feet, then walked away.[88] Jeff saw these signs and stood there until the blast tragically blew off both of his legs.[89]

Let's consider the action taken against three other seemingly reasonable courses of action.

---

85 During the 1996 summer Olympics in Atlanta, Georgia and the first of four bombings committed by Eric Robert Rudolph. The Olympic bombing killed 2 and injured 111.

86 The multi-bomb coordinated attack on the Cercanias commuter train system in Madrid, Spain killed 191 and injured over 1,800.

87 On July 7, 2005 a series of coordinated suicide attacks carried out by Islamic terrorists; four bombs were detonated aboard London Underground trains and a central London bus, killing 52 civilians and injuring over 700.

88 http://www.thesun.co.uk/sol/homepage/news/4895084/boston-bombing-victim-saw-one-of-the-attackers-drop-a-bag-at-his-feet.html

89 This is not presented in any way to second-guess Mr. Bauman's actions. Those choices and repercussions remain quite simply as a vivid case study from which we can all draw lessons to improve the way we respond in the future. The hearts of all Americans, save perhaps the scum at Rolling Stone magazine who chose to glorify the bomber like a rock star on their cover, go out to all of the victims of this tragic event.

OPTION 1. Ignore it

Conventional wisdom argues to us that the package is nothing, something inadvertently left behind by a distracted fellow traveler. After all, bombings are exceedingly rare in the United States, but they are not unheard of. Aside from major bomb attacks like the Murrah Building in Oklahoma City and the garage of the World Trade Center,[90] there have been numerous bomb attacks on places ranging from abortion clinics, airports and government buildings to a backpack bomb placed along the route of a Martin Luther King Day parade.[91] Between 1978 and 1995 "Unabomber" Ted Kaczynski carried out an unbroken campaign of sending bombs through the mail, killing three and injuring 23. Despite this history, however, the statistical chance of a bomb attack on American soil is incredibly remote. The decision to dismiss the threat entirely carries the weight of rational probability.

What if it turns out to be nothing? If you ignore it you haven't spent an erg of energy and your day goes on undisturbed.

What if it turns out to be an explosive device? By ignoring it you have done nothing to take advantage of your awareness. Failing to react to a potential hazard is functionally the same as being oblivious to it in the first place. If you ignore it, you will get hit by whatever happens next. As we saw in Boston, proximity to even a small bomb can result in death and dismemberment.

OPTION 2. Verbal Challenge

"Hey, don't leave that thing here." The words are easy to say and do not require any position of authority. Unattended bags have long been treated as hazards at airports and such a challenge would not at all appear to be unreasonable. You can loudly advise the owner that you will call 911 if he walks away and leaves it.

What if it turns out to be nothing? On one hand, the owner may either sheepishly or grudgingly pick up the bag and carry it away, eliminating the proximate threat. However, in today's easily-offended world you may unwittingly create a confrontation where none existed. There is a chance that the owner may react poorly to your intervention and create a distasteful or even threatening situation.

What if it is a bomb? Bringing sudden public attention to a placed bomb may accelerate events abruptly. Most bombs today are detonated by remote control, using parts from a cell phone or toy. The bomb's controller, (who is most likely watching) may realize that the attack is imminent and detonate the device before the rest of the crowd can scatter. Doing so may sacrifice the bomb-placer, but in the world of terrorism today those people are disposable assets who likely have little to no value to the person holding the remote.

OPTION 3. Point at the bag and yell a warning

Let's assume for a moment that you have a greater level of certainty as to the threatening nature of the backpack. Imagine for discussion that as the owner sets it on the ground the flap rolls back revealing a bundle of end-capped steel pipes with electrical wiring and a cell phone taped to the side. Nails are duct-taped to the sides. In short, you see something that is either a real bomb, or so intended to look like a real bomb that an overt reaction would be justified. You fear for yourself and everybody around you and you point at the bag and scream "BOMB - RUN!"

---

90   April 19, 1995 and Feb 26, 1993, respectively

91   Spokane, Washington on Jan 17, 2011

What if it is a bomb? Yelling "bomb" would be as close as you could get to pulling a fire alarm. On one hand there is a chance that some people would scatter[92] and any movement away from the device would begin to reduce its lethality. As mentioned previously, however, any attempt to rapidly disperse the crowd away from the device carries a risk of accelerating its detonation.

What if it turns out to be nothing? The esteemed Justice Oliver Wendell Holmes Jr. made reference to the act of "shouting 'FIRE' in a crowded theater" as an act so likely to cause harm due to panic as to be beyond the protections of free speech.[93] The act of highlighting any threat in a crowd will likely induce some level of urgency ranging from mild panic to a chaotic stampede. In the worst of cases people will fall, get trampled on or shoved into things like breakable windows. Stairwells will become huge hazards. Some people may just have a heart attack and drop dead, and others will doubtlessly come away suffering (or at least claiming) emotional and psychological harm. While you may have had the best intention and more than reasonable justification, you can and may well face criminal prosecution and civil litigation if your actions are asserted by the most loathsome of ambulance-chasers to have been reckless, or worse yet, intended to disturb the peace or incite some sort of public disturbance or panic.

OPTION 4. Check it out

If uncertainty is the problem, one alternative that comes to mind is to walk up and take a closer look. No point causing a fuss over a backpack full of dirty laundry and books, right? Sadly, this is one of those times when a normal reaction can place you at increased risk of harm. Earlier in the book we explained why you should never approach a person who threatened you, even if seemingly incapacitated. That same rule applies to unknown and unattended packages. If ignoring it is bad, getting closer to it is even worse.

Touching a suspected threat is out of the question. Some explosive devices are equipped with anti-tamper components; in simple language that is a part of the device that will make it go BOOM if you move it or try to "open the lid." Beyond design features, some explosive materials in general and improvised explosives in particular can be extremely sensitive to physical or electrostatic shock. The simple act of touching a bomb may be sufficient to cause detonation. There is an old saying that "curiosity killed the cat" but a curious self-appointed bomb-sniffer can kill himself and everyone nearby.

Using a cell phone close to a suspect package is also unsafe. It is common for bombs to be triggered by cell phones or cell phone components and using your phone can produce signals that may be misread by the bomb's triggering system as a firing command. Because they are typically hand-built, these devices can be extremely sensitive.

Lastly, the closer you are to any event, the harder you will be hit by whatever comes out of it. Distance and intervening barriers remain your best friends at all times.

What if there is no real threat? If you approach a bag or box you feel to be suspicious, you gain very little meaningful data. Even a wad of laundry on top of a bomb can provide easy camouflage against a visual inspection. Unless you intend to start opening flaps, peeling off wrappers and dumping the contents on the floor, there is little the average layman can learn about a package by getting nose-to-nose with it.

---

92   Some, but rarely even a majority. The Boston Bombing was extensively videotaped and as the world saw, even the explosions themselves did not induce an immediate reaction in a great many people very close to the event. Under sudden stress people will freeze in shock or suffer various physiological reactions such as tunnel vision, auditory exclusion (the inability to properly process sound).

93   See Schenck v. United States, 249 U.S. 47 (1919)

Worse yet, if you are discovered messing with a bag that is not a threat, you may find yourself in an uncomfortable or even violent altercation with the owner, or accused of theft or vandalism. The bottom line is that approaching an unattended object offers no meaningful reward and presents considerable risk on various levels.

What if it really is a bomb? Every step you take closer to a bomb, incendiary or any other violent device increases its ability to hurt you. You would not walk up to poke an angry rattlesnake[94] or a brazen "dynamite and alarm clock" ticking time bomb; treat unknown objects with the same level of prudent caution.

Each of the four prior options carries an unmitigated if not outright aggravated risk to your safety across physical, criminal and civil litigation levels. Simply put, they do little to make you any safer and in some choices actually increase your risk. So what choice do you have that is likely to reduce your risk without creating new ones?

OPTION 5. Walk Away and Report it

In the case of the Boston bombing, bystanders and runners a mere dozen yards away escaped injury. The bomber himself walked away to safety. That is not always the case and bombs can vary dramatically in terms of volume and explosive power, but regardless of that your mind should be focused on increasing your distance and exploiting intervening solid barriers.

Unlike a public display of alarm, your casual but purposeful departure is not likely to draw the attention of either the crowd or the potential attackers. Once you reach what you feel is a safe distance away you can calmly report your concern to a police officer (police are typically visible at large public events) or through a call to 911, but neither of these carries the risk to you of creating a public disturbance. If you have been alert to detail, you can provide descriptive information that can greatly assist police in identifying the threat and the suspected perpetrator.

What if there is no real threat? If you were wrong, you did nothing more than take a short walk. No ruckus, no scene.

What if it really is a bomb? If you were right and a threat did exist, even a short distance can make an immeasurable difference in reducing your exposure to harm. Stepping inside a solidly built building might afford additional protection from flying debris.[95] Reporting your concern to local police or security personnel AFTER you are a safe distance away will help qualified, trained and equipped authorities respond as effectively as possible.

How Far is a Safe Distance?

While walking away looks to be an easy and rational response, it raises a natural question - how far is far enough? That question was addressed by the Bureau of Alcohol, Tobacco, Firearms and Explosives and subsequently adopted by the Department of Homeland Security. That data appears on the BOMB THREAT STAND-OFF CHART that appears at right.

---

94   Well, you might not, but once again YouTube provides ample documentation of people who felt compelled to do that very thing. Search for "poke rattlesnake".

95   Although if that building has windows facing the threat, keep in mind that a shockwave can transform window glass into flying fragmentation. Moving through the building away from the threat will continue to reduce your proximate exposure.

You should focus on the red and grey columns, representing the absolute minimum distance you should put between yourself and the threat. The distance in the red column represents the critical evacuation distance even if you are inside a building. The numbers in the grey column indicate the stand-off distance if you are outdoors with no solid walls between you and the bomb. You should remember that bombs create a grave shattered glass hazard even at extreme distances and standing outside a building with windows may place you in the path of falling glass.

BOMB THREAT STAND-OFF CHART

Threat Description Improvised Explosive Device (IED)	Explosives Capacity[1] (TNT Equivalent)	Building Evacuation Distance[2]	Outdoor Evacuation Distance[3]
Pipe Bomb	5 LBS	70 FT	1200 FT
Suicide Bomber	20 LBS	110 FT	1700 FT
Briefcase/Suitcase	50 LBS	150 FT	1850 FT
Car	500 LBS	320 FT	1500 FT
SUV/Van	1,000 LBS	400 FT	2400 FT
Small Moving Van/ Delivery Truck	4,000 LBS	640 FT	3800 FT
Moving Van/ Water Truck	10,000 LBS	860 FT	5100 FT
Semi-Trailer	60,000 LBS	1570 FT	9300 FT

1. These capacities are based on the maximum weight of explosive material that could reasonably fit in a container of similar size.
2. Personnel in buildings are provided a high degree of protection from death or serious injury; however, glass breakage and building debris may still cause some injuries. Unstrengthened buildings can be expected to sustain damage that approximates five percent of their replacement cost.
3. If personnel cannot enter a building to seek shelter they must evacuate to the minimum distance recommended by Outdoor Evacuation Distance. These distance is governed by the greater hazard of fragmentation distance, glass breakage or threshold for ear drum rupture.

REMEMBER: Whatever decision you make, you should never approach, inspect or attempt to move a suspect package.

If you find yourself in the proximity of any pack, luggage, parcel or object that you perceive to carry an explosive threat, the safest option is to walk away with those you love in tow, seeking at a minimum the separation distances set forth by the DHS chart. Then advise law enforcement or building / facility security and provide them with a clear description of the device and its location.

SCENARIO: THE HOME INVASION

It is quiet, like a million nights that have gone before. Work ran late again, traffic was a bear, pretty much par for the course on a Monday. But things are quiet now; dinner plates are still in the sink but the kids are tucked in and you have a chance to read a few pages of an old paperback before calling it a night. Even the dog is at rest, sprawled across the foot of the bed making those funny grunting noises in his sleep. The house too mutters its usual odd sounds, the dull groan of settling weight or the shudder of a water pipe somewhere in the wall. You know these sounds, they are old roommates you'd just as soon not have, but long ago accepted that they had come to stay.

The crack of glass is different, sharp and brittle. You turn to listen, unsure if the sound was real or something from a drowsy half-dream. But the dog is alert as well, and he certainly wasn't having the same dream. The hackles on his neck bristle as he looks at the half-open door and chuffs. From the darkness beyond, the floor creaks...

There are few areas of personal security so utterly overrun with misconceptions and bad advice as the home invasion scenario. In our own home the normal stress regarding our safety gets further muddled by the indignation that stems from our feeling of violation. *Who the hell do you think you are coming into my house?*

Let's examine some of the popularly-held options and the likely outcomes.

OPTION 1: The Warning Shot

I lead off with this ill-conceived notion only because in February 2013, Vice President Joe Biden went on national television and said that he very explicitly instructed his wife, should she ever hear a sound around the house that might be a burglar, to shoot first and think later. With all apparent seriousness Biden stated,

"I said, 'Jill, if there's ever a problem, just walk out on the balcony here, walk out, put [up] that double barreled shotgun and fire two blasts outside the house.'"

Simply put... this is so utterly mindless that it could have only come from the mouth of a politician. First and foremost, discharging any gun into the air will throw deadly projectiles into an empty sky, but gravity will bring them back down where the rest of us live. This can be dangerous if not outright deadly to neighbors or passers-by.[96]

Secondly, the most fundamental rules of gun safety dictate that you should only fire a gun in the direction of a safe backstop, something solid that the bullet cannot penetrate.

---

96   A tragic example recently took place in the Seattle suburb of Ferndale in June of 2013 when a 23-year-old woman enjoying a backyard Father's Day BBQ was fatally struck in the chest by a bullet that literally fell from the sky. Police found the shooters, two of them convicted felons, who had been target practicing half a mile away on the far side of an adjacent river with no regard for the homes around them.

Beyond the immediate hazard to life and limb, firing a gun in such a manner will very likely constitute one or more serious crimes such as Unlawful Use of a Weapon and Reckless Endangerment.[97] If the law decides that a shot was fired to protect property rather than life, police have argued that the mitigating circumstance of self-defense does not apply and defense of property does not justify the use of lethal force. Remember, no matter what direction in which you fire a gun, you are using lethal force.

If you fire a gun outside of normal recreational use at a safe range facility or hunting location, you will almost certainly be called upon to articulate in absolutely clear and precise words why you made the decision to shoot. Taking such action for anything less than a clear, explicit threat to your life[98] carries a severe risk of criminal and civil liability that can have repercussions on your employment and financial security as well as your freedom. Being "right" in your own eyes or having good intentions will mean absolutely NOTHING if the system decides to move against you.

There are other tactical considerations that argue against the idea of a warning shot but the first two points are so utterly overwhelming as to close this discussion entirely. No matter what the Vice President says, or any other equally misguided individual, you should never, ever fire a warning shot. Ever. If you are not in immediate danger of grievous harm, do not shoot. If you are in immediate danger of grievous harm, shoot to stop the threat. Blindly firing any weapon, be it indoors or outdoors, for any reason creates a grotesque risk for harm, lawsuits and criminal charges.

What if... Nope. There is NO positive "what if" outcome for firing a warning shot. Even if a warning shot succeeds in causing a Bad Guy to run away you will have placed yourself in dire exposure for numerous life-changing hazards.

OPTION 2: Sweep the House

We have watched this scene play out in a hundred movies. Having heard the sound depicted in the scenario, the homeowner picks up a baseball bat, a golf club, perhaps even a gun, and begins to creep through darkened halls in search of the invader. Maybe he turns on lights, or proceeds in the dark. Sadly, like most things we see on our movie screens, this idea is fraught with hazards.

Police and military units study CQB, which means close-quarters battle. This is the kind of fighting that takes place proverbially nose-to-nose, firefights within a single room for example. CQB can be a brutal and unforgiving style of battle because at such short distances even a poor marksman can hit a target and combatants are close enough to use weapons like knives or baseball bats. Entry teams know that a Bad Guy can spring out of concealment and be in your face before you have a chance to react.

One of the fundamental principles of CQB is called the Fatal Funnel. When you normally enter a room you do so through a predictable path - the door. A constrained path just some 30-inches wide, a door or hallway acts as a physical bottleneck that can be readily covered.

---

97   Oregon resident Cory Thompson, a veteran of Iraq and Afghanistan, discovered a man (who later proved to be a known felon) trying to break through the door of Thompson's house. Thompson fired one round into the ground as a warning. Police arrived and confiscated the weapon and charged homeowner Thompson with Reckless Endangering, Menacing and Unlawful Use of a Firearm.

98   There are conditional circumstances in which you can receive the same self-defense protection when acting to defend the lives of others, but understand that these are not universal. Protection of family and friends is traditionally held to be part of self-defense but the extent to which you can act to defend strangers is subject to interpretation if it is felt that your actions crossed into the realm of police authority. Just because people may be in danger doesn't give you a clear right to save them, no matter how brave or well-intended that might be.

To make matters worse, you may find yourself silhouetted by any back-light as you enter the next room. Anyone lurking in a dark room has a distinct advantage over someone trying to enter through such a bottleneck.

This dynamic is one reason why police have things like "flashbang" grenades, which produce a staggering burst of light and sound that can temporarily blind and deafen people close to the grenade when it detonates. Rather than pass through the Bad Guy's Fatal Funnel, they can toss in a flashbang, break the opponent's focus and sweep into the room before he has a chance to recover.

But citizens don't usually have a flashbang on hand. As a result, when you start moving from room to room, even in your own house, you are likely conceding the advantage of Fatal Funnel to the intruder. Yes, there is a chance you might catch the dullest of criminals unaware. But the mere act of walking in most homes will produce sounds that can alert an intruder to your approach who will then remain motionless and wait for you to enter and expose yourself to sudden grievous injury.

A collateral hazard from sweeping the house becomes evident if you do not live alone. If you choose to investigate a sound, so might other members of your family, or they might want to make sure you are OK. This creates a multi-player hazard in which one or more of you can enter a Bad Guy's Fatal Funnel, or family members may surprise one another in a violent exchange borne out of stress and misguided identification. If one resident wandering through the darkness is bad, a group bumbling around in the dark is even worse.

Turning lights on as you sweep is one alternative to moving in the dark, but the successive dark-to-light cycles will ruin your night vision and diminish your ability to respond quickly to an unexpected threat. If an intruder is present, the progression of light will in most buildings cascade from room to room, warning of your approach and creating a pronounced backlight to anyone who has taken up an ambush position in a dark room. Walking from a lit room into the doorway of a dark room is the ultimate Fatal Funnel arrangement.

Yet another hazard of sweeping a house arises when you consider the factor of firearms. The walls and floors of a home may or may not stop a bullet. If you move through a house you increase the risk of encountering a Bad Guy who is now between you and your family, even if walls or even floors separate you. A bullet fired at a Bad Guy could in such a situation pass through any number of intervening things with enough force to reach a loved one. You cannot control the direction in which a Bad Guy might aim or fire a gun, but you can and should absolutely control the direction that you do. The safest way to employ any weapon is at the threat with everybody else behind you, ideally behind solid cover.

But the greatest hazard of a sweep is actually finding an intruder, or perhaps more than one. Now you are both in a room together, face-to-face. You may have a weapon, they may as well. What now? Do you scream at them to leave, or perhaps try to somehow wrestle them into some sort of detainment? Or do things simply break down into an all-out fight?

The sad truth is that you don't get to make that call. You may want only to order the intruders from your home but they may decide, logically or otherwise, that their best interests lie in injuring or even killing you. They may have intended to hurt you in the first place. Or in rare instances they may be in your home by some mistake, maybe looking for help, maybe drunk, yet in whatever diminished mental state perceive your appearance with bat or gun in hand as a threat to them. By sweeping the house you have potentially moved yourself into direct proximity with an unknown threat who may have the upper hand at the moment of contact. You have thrown wide the doors to civil and criminal liability and done little to improve your personal safety.

What if... you sweep and nobody is there? Sneaking about in the dark, even in your own home, is not an altogether safe activity. While we all think we have a perfect mental map, invariably the ottoman is not where we remembered it, the toy truck is on the floor; there are a hundred ways in a darkened house to trip or get injured. Stairs are a notable hazard when moving around in the dark. Falling, especially with a weapon in hand, creates a hazard of being hurt in multiple ways.

What if... you sweep and an intruder IS there? The risks of a sweep are numerous, to include actually finding the person for whom you went looking. If your defensive strategy is being The Bear, (i.e. you are counting on your ability to fight as a preferred method of defense,) this may well be a situation when you will be forced to put that ability to the test. If you have a weapon you have put yourself in a situation most likely to require you to employ it. You have reduced the window of time for police to arrive and intervene, or for medical units to arrive in time to save you from injuries should they be inflicted. If you have loved ones elsewhere in the house you have greatly increased the risk that the use of a firearm, by anybody involved, will randomly punch through floors or walls in their direction. You sacrifice position, the element of surprise, the Fatal Funnel and any benefits of fortification by moving into an undefined encounter.

OPTION 3: Fortify and call for help

After looking at the risks of Options 1 and 2, it should seem pretty clear that what we really want (well, besides wanting the Bad Guy to simply leave on his own) is to limit any ability to reach you and control the terms of an encounter. Ideally we want to stall that encounter until the police can arrive but if that ultimately proves impossible, we want the Bad Guy to walk into our Fatal Funnel. We don't want to walk into his. We want all of our loved ones behind us so that if we have to use force of any kind, and especially a gun, family members are not downrange.

Consider this addition: our scenario takes place in an average family home of two parents and two kids, where each kid has a room. Whichever parent is the Primary Defender grabs the weapon of choice and takes a position at the Fatal Funnel point that separates the sleeping area from the rest of the house. [99] The other parent quickly grabs both kids and all four of you retreat into a bedroom that you have decided provides the best security. [100] You close and lock the bedroom door, retreat to the opposite side of the room and call 911. The Primary Defender maintains a strict focus on the bedroom door, which has become the new Fatal Funnel. The other parent handles the 911 call and makes sure that neither kid strays out into the potential battlespace.

There are a number of very tangible benefits from this strategy. First is that you are all together and nobody is wandering around bumping into an invader in the dark. If there is only one way into your place of refuge you have a clear Fatal Funnel. You have the flexibility to position the Primary Defender at a distance and angle best suited for whatever weapon has been selected. [101] You have the added option of shoving anything solid, like a dresser, against the door to further bolster its value as a barricade.

---

99   Typical home design tends to sequester bedrooms from the primary living space through some sort of hallway, doorway or a staircase in the event of a multi-level home. If there is only one way to get into the bedroom area from the remainder of the house, this type of structural bottleneck can provide your first Fatal Funnel.

100   Factors that affect the choice might be things like a brick or solid timber wall unique to one room. If you have planned for a Fortify strategy, your refuge may have such simple benefits as a solid wood door (which is considerably stronger than a typical hollow-core door that can be easily splintered) as well as an interior deadbolt lock. A solid locking door can add considerably to the time needed to make forced entry and delay the advance of the threat.

101   To either side of the door if you rely on things like a baseball bat or a knife, or ideally from behind solid cover if you have a gun.

If the door is locked, an assailant will have to break it down to get at you. Oddly enough, this accomplishes a couple of things, the first being simple delay. In a perfect world your fortification will hold up long enough for police to arrive and free you from having to fight. If police do not arrive in time, the physical assault on the door itself leaves a clear demonstration of the intent of the Bad Guy to cause harm.[102] There may be any number of reasons a stranger inadvertently ends up in your house, but only one reason they would beat down a locked bedroom door. While secondary in timeliness to physical safety, ongoing protection from criminal and civil liability remains a very real concern in any altercation. As a strategy, Fortify gives you a lot of support to "be right" at the end of the day.

At a final level, a solid door is less likely to fail abruptly which means that an assailant can be forced to remain largely in place trying to break into the room. This situation can increase the lethality of the Fatal Funnel, depending on the weapon(s) you may have available. If you have a gun of a caliber sufficient to penetrate a wooden door[103] you have the option of firing through the door while the assailant tries to break through it.

Case Study: Kendra St. Clair
As reported in the *New York Daily News*[104] on October 20, 2012, then 12-year-old Kendra St. Clair of Calera, Oklahoma was home alone when 32-year-old Stacey Jones banged on her door repeatedly. Fearful for her safety, the sixth-grader called her mother who instructed Kendra to get the family handgun and take refuge in a bathroom closet. Kendra did so, then called 911 as Jones broke through the back door of the house.

Kendra remained on the phone with 911 for six minutes while Jones rummaged through the house. Kendra then heard the bathroom light flip on and saw the handle of the closet door begin to turn. Although Jones was older and larger, he had walked into Kendra's Fatal Funnel and she fired one round through the door, directly above the turning door handle. The 40 caliber round struck Jones in the chest. Badly injured, he fled from the house. When Bryan County police officers arrived on the scene they were able to hunt Jones down and place him under arrest. No charges were filed against Kendra, who was hailed by police as showing remarkable poise under threat and acting in a very responsible manner.

Case Study: Zoey Ripple
On May 23, 2012, a 21-year-old University of Colorado student named Zoey Ripple entered the home of Timothy Justice and Doreen Orion. As reported in the Boulder Daily Camera[105] Justice awoke to find Ripple standing in their bedroom holding a light. Justice stated that Ripple did not say a word as he repeatedly told her to get out of the house, and that she continued to advance even after he told her he had a gun. When she closed to within six feet, Justice fired one round that struck her in the hip.

102　Bad Guys have argued a million reasons they were found inside somebody's home. I was drunk, I got lost, somebody gave me a wrong address. While the mere presence of an uninvited stranger in your home may strike you as threatening -- and they may outright threaten you -- they will tell a wildly different story when the police do arrive and courts all too often have taken the word of a criminal over a homeowner.

103　Defensive calibers employed by law enforcement personnel, such as 9mm or .45ACP are both likely to be up to the task, with numerous options of ammunition type within each caliber.

104　http://www.nydailynews.com/news/national/home-girl-12-shoots-intruder-article-1.1188229

105　http://www.dailycamera.com/boulder-county-news/ci_21739419/zoey-ripple-plea-drunken-trespassing-case-boulder-cu?IA-DID=Search-www.dailycamera.com-www.dailycamera.com

In this case the intruder pleaded guilty to criminal trespass and no charges were filed against the homeowner under the logic that citizens have the right to defend themselves in their home. But unlike the case of Kendra St. Clair, the facts of this case are a bit less clear. It has been asserted, and remains undetermined at this time, that Ms. Ripple may have been under the influence of alcohol or a date-rape drug that left her in a diminished mental state. She had no criminal record and nothing beyond her presence in the house suggested that she intended harm to the residents.

The question of her intent may never be answered conclusively but it raises a different "what if" point that touches on any defensive act. What if Ms. Ripple was herself a victim, confused and looking for help? What if the homeowners had instead fled to a bathroom and braced the door before deciding to shoot?

Some are quick to debate the "duty to retreat" as though it were a debt owed to the assailant. Statements like "I am in my home, I don't have to back up" are commonly-heard retorts to the notion of backing away from a criminal threat. Depending on your jurisdiction, that may or may not be true. Terms like "castle doctrine" refer to a variety of laws that define how your self-defense actions may be perceived by a court of law after the event is over. In some areas where castle doctrine is in effect, citizens may have little to no obligation to try to retreat or escape before employing force in their defense. In others, however, the legal protections of self-defense may be limited if a citizen did not first demonstrate reasonable, or perhaps even unreasonable efforts to run away before using force as a defense.

At the end of the day, however, it is no fun to hurt somebody else, much less to take a human life, even to save your own life. The decision to put a bullet in somebody, or to bash someone with a baseball bat, can leave scars that some people carry forever. Arguably, harm is better given than received but the gravity of that choice should, to the rational mind, elevate the benefits of Fortify if for no other reason than to forestall the need for a violent response.

Your decision when to run and when to stand your ground may be affected by numerous factors. If you are protecting others who cannot run, flight may not be an option. If you are less mobile, fighting at the time and place that favors you may be the only logical decision. In some cases running may involve abandoning a location that offers greater protection than the initial line of flight; thus getting caught "out in the open" might be worse than remaining in place.

No book can foresee the future and give you some universal rule to govern these decisions. This is where strategies like Fortify, when available, can provide a significant benefit. In cases where the intent of the intruder is not clear, or may be construed differently in a court of law months later, a complete defensive strategy should seek to provide you with safety-enhancing options you can exercise before taking an act that cannot be undone. When shot, Ms. Ripple was severely injured and left with medical repercussions she may carry for the rest of her life. A different type of injury could have proved fatal.

Since I wasn't there, I do not presume to second-guess Mr. Justice as to the danger he may have perceived. There is never perfect knowledge of any situation. The decision to use deadly force of any kind is a weighty one and each individual should be absolutely clear as to a personal threshold for taking action against a threat, and articulating that logic in the processes to follow.

Myth: "...drag them back inside"
We have all heard the old adage, "If you have to shoot somebody in your house and they make it out alive, drag them back inside before the cops show up." This silly fable stems from the notion that self-defense within your home is different from the same action taken outside and that police will be unable to detect the movement. This "myth-conception" is completely and utterly wrong on numerous levels.

Law enforcement personnel don't need a high-tech CSI team to see that a crime scene has been altered, especially very gross changes like moving a body that may well have been bleeding at the time. Altering the scene of a crime to mislead police may in and of itself result in criminal charges, even if everything you did up to that point was otherwise lawful.

Equally unwise is that if you attempt to move a body you must approach it, which violates the concrete safety rule about staying away from an assailant until police arrive to secure the scene. Someone you believe to be dead may actually be alive; moving "the body" can expose you to danger or lead to further injury and even death, resulting to untold criminal and civil exposures.

While commonly heard and thought to be sound guidance by a frightening number of people, the notion of moving anything at a crime scene, especially moving what may or may not be an incapacitated assailant, places you at extreme risk of physical harm, criminal prosecution and civil liability. NEVER approach a fallen assailant, regardless of condition or location. If you believe that an active criminal threat has ceased to be active for any reason or duration, take that time to get away from it, find safe refuge and call 911.

SCENARIO: THE WORKPLACE SHOOTER

It has been a tough day at the office. Every day since the furloughs were handed out things have been tougher and tougher on the survivors. Naturally, nobody decreased the workload and now 32 people have to do the work of 45. Tensions have been running high. To make matters worse, the AC has been stuttering in the summer heat. You look at the clock and wish for the hundredth time today that you had called in sick.

Suddenly there's a commotion in the front office, was that a scream? Then the door swings open abruptly as a disheveled man walks in, turning straight towards the executive offices. He looks like Dave, a Director in Marketing, a quiet guy by most accounts, maybe a little high strung. But Dave shouldn't be here now; he was one of the dozen that got a pink slip last week. As Dave marches past a row of cubes, grumbling incoherently, you see what looks like a shotgun in his hand...

The scenario of an armed attack on an office, school, theater or church is perhaps the most difficult one for most Americans to imagine, and the most foreign to our traditional way of thinking. Because these events erupt without warning in settings that seem removed from violent thought, they carry a stunning suddenness that can overwhelm the ability of the unprepared to respond. These scenarios can place citizens in the worst of all places - crowded in close proximity to an assailant where options are greatly restricted. Quick and decisive action can be critical in these situations.

Let's take a look at our options here in explicit terms of the Four F's and what kinds of results we have seen when they have been applied in actual active shooter events.

Option 1: Feign - Play Dead or Play Gone

In the chaos of an attack on a crowd, especially one that involves numerous injuries and a crowded environment, somewhat different opportunities to Feign become viable. In the chaos, one might disappear or play dead.

In a multi-room environment such as an office, school or church, people may be caught within the incident yet not immediately observed by the assailants. In such a scenario, a reactive Feign tactic may buy time for the cavalry to arrive. An assailant who remains unaware of your presence will spend no energy trying to find you.

At the onset of commotion, it may be possible to hide in an out-of-the-way location. Turning off the lights and locking any intervening doors can help to sell the illusion that your refuge was left unoccupied. Minimizing your signature (any action that draws attention to your location) is critical for this subterfuge to work. A cell phone ringing or the screen of a smartphone suddenly lighting up can draw further investigation.

If the option presents itself, refuge next to a solid barrier may provide additional protection from stray bullets. A filled bookcase or file cabinet presents considerable material through which a bullet must pass.

As mentioned earlier in the book, camouflage or hiding is an all-or-nothing gambit but in a chaotic active shooter scenario it is typical for assailants to focus on the greatest number of targets in the shortest time. It is not typical for a shooter to exhaust effort on a door-to-door search when other targets are readily identified.

Playing dead is an even more expedient form of Feign. Should you find yourself in the same room as a shooter with no way to get to an exit or cover, flopping down on the ground may cause you to be overlooked. Sadly, this gambit is most effective when other members of the crowd have fallen.

This strategy was employed successfully by victims of the 2012 theater shooting in Aurora, Colorado as well as individuals caught in the Trident Hotel during the Mumbai mass terrorist attack of 2008. For those who find themselves unexpectedly in the forefront of a large attack, or those with very limited mobility, hiding or playing dead can be a reasonable choice in the absence of better alternatives.

Option 2: Fortress - Lockdown

Lockdown is a highly likely response to attacks on most schools and some places of work. The idea behind Lockdown is to compartmentalize a target-rich environment and force an assailant to consume as much time as possible moving from one target group to the next. It is based on the premise that police will in fact be storming in to respond and that in an extremely short response time, every moment of delay has significant impact. The increasing presence of police officers on school grounds, or added patrols in the vicinity of schools, can greatly reduce the normal time required to bring an armed response to the scene.

The effectiveness of this strategy will hinge in large part on the ability of a room to serve as a Fortress. While average classroom doors may not be designed to withstand a great deal of force, the delay can keep an assailant in an otherwise empty hallway, thereby apt to be more readily spotted and engaged by responding officers. To extend this time, the durability of a door might be enhanced by such ad hoc measures as shoving a teacher's desk against the inside of the door, or any collection of heavy objects like file cabinets, bookshelves or lab tables. For example, things students carry, like bicycle cable locks, might be useful in further securing the door or joining individual barricade items into a fused and more immovable mass.

Within the Fortress, anything that can personally be used as body armor may reduce the chance of being injured by a stray or ricochet. As mentioned earlier, professional products such as backpacks lined with Kevlar are readily available, but other things common in a classroom can be very good bullet-stops. Books are difficult to penetrate and a stack of them can add a measurable amount of ad hoc cover. An overturned solid wood lab table or bookcase might stop a bullet or at least peel off a portion of the bullet's energy and mass. In short, anything that can be interposed between victims and the threat should be exploited.

As a determined assailant may fire at a door lock in an attempt to break it, victims may be at greater risk gathering in a straight line through the door. If the door or wall has a window that affords a view of the room, any measure to obstruct that view can help reduce the ability of a shooter to see and aim at targets, even if firing through the wall or door itself. Items common to many classrooms, such as an American flag or student posters, could be used as an ad hoc window cover.

Option 3: Flight

We know that distance and barriers are our friends, so logic says that if we have a shooter inside the building, the best place we can be is outside the building and moving away. This creates a challenge for individuals, be they students, faculty or parents, who wish to follow this path but are told that remaining in place is school policy. Knowing the policy of your school or workplace in advance will allow you to better understand those options and either address the policy administratively or formulate your plan to act otherwise. You should reflect on your feelings about any attempt to force you into action or inaction, if you reasonably believe that doing so will lead to the death of you or a loved one.

Flight is most effective when executed quickly, before a hostile force has the opportunity to secure control of the building. If you choose Flight, you should take the shortest route out of the building and keep running once you are outside; in an active shooter scenario bullets may be coming out through windows or walls. Take nothing; packs and parcels can slow your ability to run and may be misconstrued as dangerous objects.

Moving through a hallway en route to an exit may carry the risk of running headlong into an assailant so you should use your ears as well as your eyes to be aware of the corridor ahead of you. It may also result in running into armed police, who may mistake you for an assailant. It may in the worst of all cases put you square in-between the actual assailant and responding officers, where you will obstruct police ability to engage and potentially be exposed to fire from one or both sides.

As with any up-close encounter, Flight or Fight is a very personal decision. Body armor options such as those described earlier can help mitigate the risk of a stray round while fleeing the area.

If your room has a window and you can see outside, you can better assess your chances of running into a shooter on the way out. The window itself may serve as an escape route; under imminent threat of violence the prospect of getting in trouble for smashing a window with a chair is probably not your biggest worry. In the case of the Columbine school shooting the nation watched one young man, his arm broken, escape the building by crawling out of a second-floor window. The fall carried a threat of injury but evidently, under the circumstances, that young man deemed it less dangerous than staying inside.

If you hear shooting immediately outside your room, there is considerable risk with Flight. Stepping out of a sealed space into an active battle area is highly dangerous. But if the sounds of attack are in the distance, there is a rational argument for getting out before trouble works its way to your room.

Option 4: Fight

An active shooter scenario presents different challenges than most other clashes with an armed assailant. Due to the nature of an active shooter event you will typically face mobile attackers trying to shift their attention from one target to the next while rapidly expending ammunition as opposed to an attacker fixated on a single target. They typically carry multiple weapons and may transition between them without warning. Nonetheless, their need to re-load may create windows of opportunity to launch a counter-attack. Their tendency to move through a kill zone may carry them into your Fatal Funnel, in this case any location that allows you to strike suddenly from a range that favors whatever weapon is at your disposal.

Any attempt to engage an active shooter should be done to inflict grievous injury that will result in immediate de-animation. It should be carried out suddenly and brutally. There is no "nice way" to injure another person. Keep in mind that attacking a violent Bad Guy will put you at the center of his radar. Any violent capacity you fail to disable will be used against you with ferocity.

If you have to fight someone who has a gun, logic says you should have a gun yourself. That is the only weapon that can match an assailant's ability to project force over distance. The strength of a gun is its ability to de-animate an opponent with as little as one well-placed shot.

The liability of having a gun is that you will doubtlessly face the prospect of criminal charges and civil liability if anything arising from your pulling the trigger in fact, or in assertion, causes harm to anybody else. If you miss, you can hit somebody else. If you hit the assailant and the bullet passes through them, you can hit somebody else. If police or other responders come through the door and see you shooting, they may mistake you for the Bad Guy. None of these are trivial outcomes; in fact any one can be devastating.

On the other hand, allowing an active shooter to continue his rampage may well result in many more people killed or injured. Ultimately, only you can decide what steps you will take and what risk you will incur to protect yourself, your loved ones or total strangers.

Creativity in selecting an improvised weapon can pay dividends. A fire extinguisher, for example, can be gripped by the handle and swung with considerable force. Dumbbells in a gym can also add bone-crushing impact to an otherwise unremarkable physical blow. The biology room in a school may well have sharp implements used for dissection, just as a woodshop might have a hammer. As demonstrated routinely in America's prisons, even a simple broom-handle (or wooden flagpole) can be snapped with a stomp, producing what amounts to a long wooden stake that can be thrust with deadly effect.

Separating an opponent from a weapon is another important goal in any confrontation. If a shooter drops his gun he becomes "just a guy" that can be fought by more conventional means. Taking up a fallen weapon[106], kicking it away or otherwise making it irretrievable or unserviceable will help mitigate the risk from that assailant.

Active shooter scenarios raise another challenge with respect to last-moment decisions. A strong defensive measure against an armed Bad Guy may stagger him or cause him to drop his weapon. This in turn may create an opportunity to break away, or to inflict greater injury and leave the assailant more thoroughly incapacitated. There is no book that can tell you the right answer, but let's look at choices in general.

Running away may increase your chances of escape if the shooter is more than momentarily disabled. On the other hand, a Bad Guy might recover quickly from an injury; he may pick up a dropped weapon or take up another one. The possibilities, good and bad, are limitless.

Trying to restrain a Bad Guy is an alternative which, in theory, may allow you to control an opponent without gravely injuring him. Few people keep handcuffs around, but things like duct tape, rope or zip ties have been successfully used to immobilize an attacker for a limited duration. In certain aircraft incidents, passengers used seat belts to help restrain an overpowered threat.

Be aware, this is a risky course of action that demands remaining in proximity with the Bad Guy. It is no small matter to hog-tie someone who doesn't want to be tied up. Keep in mind that confinement may be an acceptable form of short-term restraint. If separated from weapons, an assailant locked in a car trunk or solid room may have little ability to threaten anyone. But a lot of modern construction, especially internal walls made of materials like drywall, are little more than cosmetic dividers. A lot of folks could kick their way through a drywall enclosure in very little time.

Violence is the final resort. Passengers on a Southwest airlines flight headed for Salt Lake City in September 2000 were stunned when passenger Jonathan Burton tried to kick in the cockpit door. A group of passengers subdued Burton and beat him to death. In July 2012 six Muslim hijackers tried to seize a Tianjin Airlines flight and passengers beat two of them to death as well. One can debate the moral implications forever but the practical result is undeniable, in each case noted above the threat ended conclusively.

---

106   There is a risk with taking up an opponent's weapon in an active shooter scenario. Response teams may be inbound looking for something no more specific than "some guy with a rifle." If you are holding that rifle when police enter the door it is not just likely, but almost certain, that you will be taken for one of the assailants.

One must always keep in mind that violence is a slippery slope. A victim who has not previously experienced mortal combat will be hard-pressed to keep a clear head in a time like this; emotions like fear and anger can merge into an adrenaline-fueled blur. Under such stress, we lose fine motor skills and tend to hit harder than we might expect. People in the grip of panic may not stop when calmer heads might say the fight has been won. Training, practice and mental preparation are important to your performance in a violent conflict.

As to your decision in any given moment I can offer only this final bit of analysis: if you "have your opponent down and let him go" you may face the prospect of the Bad Guy regrouping and continuing his assault. This carries one set of physical dangers to everyone at the scene and lays a minefield of psychological and emotional hazards. If on the other hand you make a concerted effort to "put him down for good" you may face a different set of dangers or have to deal with the consequences - from legal to psychological - that stems from outcomes such as taking a human life or inflicting permanent injury. How you act at such a moment will likely hinge on a combination of your unique physical, emotional and human values.

SCENARIO: KIDNAP or CARJACK

The elevator opens and you walk across the near-empty lobby, tossing a goodnight wave to Bob at the security desk. He's a nice guy, forced by a bad economy to spend his retirement years parked in front of a bank of TV monitors that give him a view from half a dozen closed circuit cameras. He'd rather be fishing, a point he mentions often. You glance at your watch as you exit the building and trudge down the block to your car. Today was a good day for parking, you lucked into a spot by the coffee shop less than a hundred yards away. Your briefcase thuds on the roof of the car as you fish for your keys when a figure emerges from the shadows and steps up to the passenger-side door. It takes a second for your brain to register the gun in his hand, dull silver catching the glare of the streetlight. He makes a sharp downward motion towards the car and growls: Get in...

This is the opening scene of any number of kidnap or carjack situations. The criminal seeks to force your compliance through the display of force, rather than the outright use of force on the spot. It is regarding that very hesitance that must give conscious thought.

If we slip into "why" we might ask ourselves why a Bad Guy would want to take us someplace else? If they wanted to take your valuables, they could do so on the spot. If they wanted the keys, you could hand them over. If they want to hurt you, even kill you, they can use whatever weapon they have in hand right here and now.

There are only three solid reasons to take you to a different location. One is arguably to access an ATM machine to secure money you don't have on hand, but they can just as easily demand your PIN number and do that without you. Hauling you to an ATM for what is typically a $300 to $500 limited withdrawal seems paltry reward for risking a kidnap charge, although criminals have kidnapped and murdered for far less.

The second reason is a straightforward kidnap scenario, where you will be held for some sort of ransom. If you are not notably affluent, or you are not traveling in a foreign nation, the odds of being targeted for a planned kidnap attempt are rather remote. But in any case, the risks associated with a kidnap, even if the intent is ransom, are considerable. There have been many cases where the kidnappers have not only abused but ultimately killed the hostage to minimize the chances of later being identified.

The only remaining reason to take you to a different location is to hurt you longer and more slowly than they can where you stand. This new location is called a Secondary Crime Scene and it is where some of the most horrific, sadistic of crimes take place.

You do not, under any circumstances, want to allow yourself to be taken to another destination.

A Secondary Crime Scene is guaranteed to be:

1)   hand-picked by the criminal to be out of sight and out of earshot

2)   by remoteness or by fortification (the bad kind) a location that will limit your ability to escape

3)   somewhere the criminal will feel empowered to do to you whatever he wants, for as long as it amuses him.

Consider the several cases in recent years where young women have escaped from imprisonment. Some had been held for periods of ten years or more, in basement dungeons hidden beneath suburban homes. These women were held in sunless rooms and subjected to years of rape, torture and neglect as well as in some cases childbirth and the death of those children. It sounds like the makings of a B-grade horror movie until you see it on the evening news in an average town in America.

But not all Secondary Crime Scenes are intended for long-term confinement. In April of 2013, two men (one of whom was a high school librarian) were arrested by the FBI for their efforts to kidnap, torture and murder women as a way of acting out their violent fantasies. These were not idle thoughts. The two had amassed a stockpile of equipment that ranged from Tasers and restraints to skewers and dental retractors - tools for removing teeth.

On January 29, 2013, Jimmy Lee Dykes boarded a Dale County school bus, killed the driver and kidnapped a 5-year old boy. He took the child to a bunker that he had constructed in the woods. One can only imagine what someone has in mind when they build an underground bunker in the woods in preparation for kidnapping a child. In that instance, police were able to follow Dykes. They stormed the bunker, killed Dykes and rescued the child. This was a truly rare event: an overwhelming majority of cases that move to a remote secondary scene end in the worst possible ways.

Even if an assailant is armed with a gun, as we depict in our scenario, police around the country agree that you are better off trying to run than you are allowing yourself to be abducted. In fact, law enforcement has developed a model called the 50-50 rule as a way of looking very informally at the comparative chances of survival through taking action on the street. The model presumes a felon with a gun has, for rough estimation, an equal 50-50 chance of either outcome through four stages of an escape. The model works like this:

1. If you run, there is a 50-50 chance the felon will shoot at all. Firing a gun in public can draw a lot of unwanted attention. Bob, our security guard, is just one of many people who may be within earshot of a scream or a gun being fired. That's why the criminal wants to take you somewhere else in the first place.

2. An attacker shooting at a moving target has a 50-50 chance of hitting you at all.

3. If you are hit, there is a 50-50 chance it will be a serious injury.

4. If you are seriously injured, there is a 50-50 chance it will be fatal.

When you string those events together you see a rapidly decreasing probability of death. Calculated as a simplistic sequential probability, step 1 carries a 50% chance, step 2 drops to 25%, step 3 falls to 12.5% leaving a 6.25% chance of fatality. While very broad in nature, this probability flies against the almost absolute certainty of horrific injury or death to those who are carted away.

To further support an escape decision, those who are injured on a public street are likely to draw police and medical aid, while those injured in a basement or some distant forest may go unnoticed for days or months or forever. One might grimly point out that in the worst case outcomes where fatal injuries are inflicted, the victims will at least be found promptly and their loved ones spared the agony of a protracted disappearance.

There is no scenario that favors allowing your abduction. Faced with that decision you should run, fight, scream at the top of your lungs. If wrestled towards a vehicle you should kick, claw, bite or leverage any weapon within reach. If you can throw something through a storefront window you might set off an alarm. There is no legal or civil trouble you can face for making a ruckus that could be worse than the risk of being kidnapped by a violent criminal.

If you are driving a vehicle and a carjacker tries to force his way in, one option is simply to bail out, especially if you are in a populated area. Unless you have loved ones in the car, there is nothing more important than gaining separation from the attacker and the more unexpected your change of direction, the more effective it is likely to be. You can also use the physics of the car itself to your advantage. A motor vehicle is a huge heavy object of considerable power and can prove very hazardous to somebody trying to climb in without your consent. Sideswiping a vehicle or building may tear your passenger door off, but it will also have a sudden impact on an attacker trying to get in. In an open area, a sudden surge in reverse, especially where the open door may knock the intruder to the ground, can also interrupt any entry into the vehicle.

Carrying this line of thought to its full extent, if you have knocked an assailant to the ground and you are in control of a moving vehicle, your most direct action would then be to drive away to a safe refuge and call 911. There is very little that an unarmed, on-foot assailant, or one who is armed with a knife or bat, can do to a car driving away. If the assailant has a gun however, there is a chance of a shot being fired at your vehicle. There are an infinite number of variables that could affect your decision at that moment but it bears mention that an armed carjacker who you may have just knocked down remains a real threat to your safety. Driving over, as opposed to around, such a threat is likely to further diminish any ability it has to hurt you.

SCENARIO: CROWD VIOLENCE

It was supposed to be a vacation, just a few precious summer days with the family taking in the sights. The day started at the mall, then meandered over to putt-putt golf. Everybody was having a good time, laughing and teasing as you walked out to the car. Traffic seemed oddly congested as you pulled out into the street. Cars were backed up in different directions and foot traffic was heavy. Before you knew it, more cars had pulled up behind you and a turn-around became very difficult. Voices ahead were loud, you couldn't make out the words but the sound carried the beat of a chanted cadence. Some kind of protest. Something about justice. Nervously, you locked the door.

A thought flickered in the back of your mind, images of the highly charged court case that had filled the TV day in and day out. It had gone to the jury just a day ago, maybe two. Had they reached a decision? Then somebody screamed several cars ahead, followed by the sound of breaking glass. Objects were hurled and looking down the line of cars you now saw people fighting in the streets. The commotion was rolling this way...

In most of the scenarios we have thus far explored, the presence of people is looked at as a positive thing. Be they protectors or merely witnesses, a crowd will typically offer some measure of deterrence to a lone criminal, or even to a small group. But what happens when the crowd is the danger? What happens when the ugly violence of mob mentality overwhelms social behavior? In those instances, humans can be their most inhuman to one another.

Against an angry crowd, most man-portable weapons are very ineffective. Consider for a moment the limited power of entire lines of police in full armor, carrying shields and batons. They can at best hold a line against a rioting crowd and in many cases can be rapidly swarmed over. Driving back a violent crowd often entails the use of considerable force such as fire hoses or tear gas. Civilians under most situations will not have weapons such as these.

When compared to a human being, or even a mob of human beings, a motor vehicle offers a tremendous physics advantage in terms of speed and mass. In times of threat from crowd violence, this advantage can be a powerful defensive weapon if you can overcome the road-safety rules that have been driven into our heads since our teen years.

Earlier in this book we examined the fate of Reginald Denny who tragically allowed himself to be dragged from the cab of an 18-wheeler that had more than enough power to drive through, or over, the crowd around him. This book does not presume to second-guess someone in a crisis nor to diminish the alternative impact on Mr. Denny's life if he had crushed a dozen people to death driving out of his situation. Life serves up tests that offer no easy answers.

What this book will point out simply, is that human beings on foot do not have the ability to physically stop a moving motor vehicle. Multiple impacts to the front grill may damage the radiator and ultimately cause the engine to overheat in time, but at a modest forward speed (or driven in reverse and leading with the trunk) a car or truck can plow through a great many threats. That action may result in lawsuits or criminal prosecution; had Mr. Denny not been beaten on live TV lawyers after the fact would most certainly argue he never was in any real danger.

If you find yourself in a bad roadway situation, stay in your vehicle and keep the engine running with your windows up. If at all possible, move away from the threat the moment you feel uncomfortable. It is better to drive miles out of your way than to knowingly or unwittingly drive into the middle of a dangerous crowd scenario. Keep in mind that other vehicles around you may also respond unexpectedly to the same threats, producing very abnormal car behavior. This can endanger you directly or can further enflame a crowd into indiscriminate violence. Whatever the progression of events, keep in mind that your vehicle represents a powerful choice in terms of evading a hazard that threatens to surround you and prevent your escape.

Similar to a riot but much smaller in scale are Road Rage events. Road Rage is a dangerous public tantrum, a narcissistic fit of fury carried out in a motor vehicle. While pathetic and illegal, these assaults can be dangerous and Road Ragers will cut others off, brake abruptly in front of them or even ram their cars intentionally. Should you be the victim of such an event, you should remember two important things:

First is that a collision which in another context would merely be a traffic accident is, if committed intentionally, a form of vehicular assault. Somebody bumping a car into yours in a lunatic fit is subjecting you to far greater deadly force than firing a gun in your direction. Your ability to respond in self-defense starts the moment somebody begins threatening behavior like swerving in front of you or trying to force you to stop.

Although it is our common training to stop when we have a collision, you should not stop if you are the victim of a Road Rage attack. History has shown that people who stop in such instances then find themselves confronted with their attacker standing at the driver's door. It is not considered "leaving the scene of an accident" to move away from what you perceive as an ongoing violent assault. It is important, however, that you call the police as quickly as possible. Drive at a controllable speed until you find a police officer or can pull into a well-lit, populated area and call 911.

The final form of crowd violence is thankfully the most rare, but a scenario of extremely complex dynamics. This is the large-scale organized attack.

Case study: Mumbai 2008
In the dark of night on November 26, 2008, members of the Lashkar-e Taiba Islamist terrorist group began a series of twelve bomb and shooting attacks spread across the city of Mumbai. The attacks were well planned, supported by detailed advance intelligence. The perpetrators were trained and well armed. Violence overwhelmed the city with a focus on locations frequented by Western tourists. I was privileged to be among a team of professionals headquartered in Huntsville, AL who were called in to respond. For the next 44 hours we led a crisis management effort for a major international firm with a dozen employees trapped in the middle of ground zero. The level of threat and highly fluid dynamics demanded innovation and an unhesitant exploitation of every possible resource. Assailants blended among the civilian population and threats appeared from every imaginable angle as police, military and even civilians brought various levels of energy into the scenario. When the smoke cleared, we brought all of our people home unharmed.

Options: Get Out or Lock Up

There is no safe way to remain outside in the midst of a riot scenario. The staggering dynamics of a large crowd present untold dangers, both from the crowd as well as the responders trying to quell the violence. If you are caught in a sudden riot scenario, or even a crowd that seems to be getting out of hand, you should leave the area or, if that is not possible, seek refuge inside of a solid structure. Move as far as possible from the threat and if you find yourself without an avenue of escape remember the lessons of the active shooter scenario. Combine Feign and Fortify by taking refuge in as safe a place as you can find, locking doors and shutting out lights to give the appearance the room is empty. In a conventional hotel room, one of the safest places to bunker down is a steel bathtub, which may provide some additional protection from bullets or fragments coming through the wall. Blankets or any other dense covering pulled over you can add to that layer of protection. If possible, try to note a room number, or in the very least a floor number, of your location. In the event of a serious incident such as this it will be critical to manage not only your avoidance of violent criminals, but your encounter with police as well.

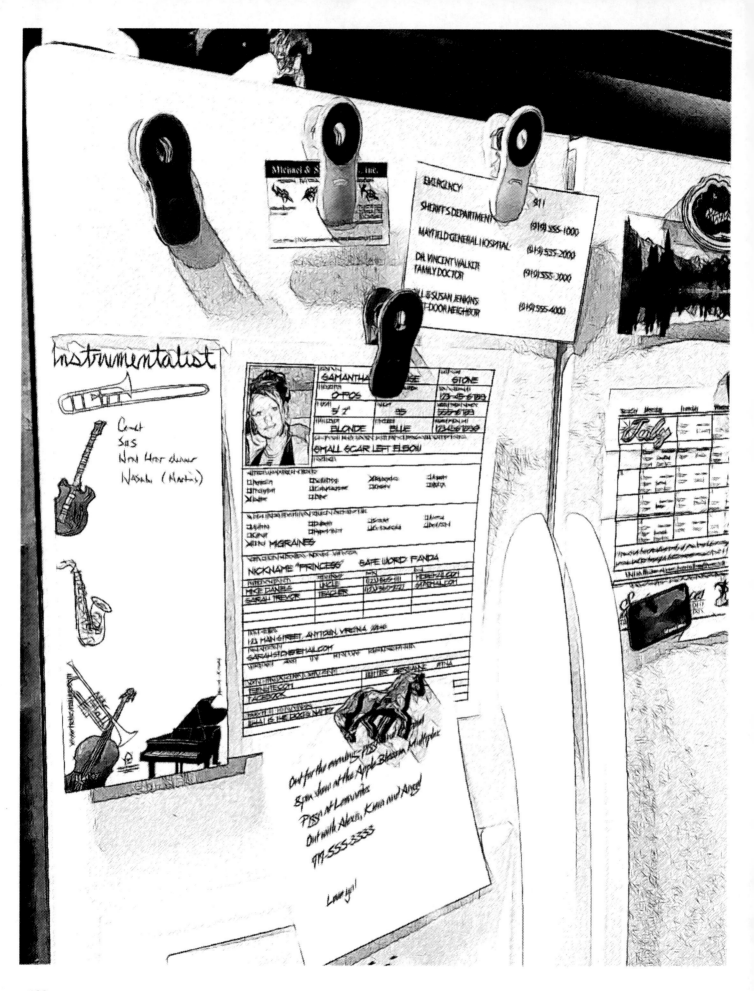

PROACTIVE MEASURES

"The secret of getting ahead is getting started."
-Mark Twain

There are some things that we can do as a normal part of our day that can help mitigate our risks or improve the response time when things go awry. These are free, minimal-effort steps that with a bit of forethought can be incorporated into our daily routines.

File a Flight Plan

We are more connected with one another today than at any other time in history. Most Americans have cell phones that can place a call from one end of the country to another. We can take photos and send them straight onto the internet for millions to see. And yet, day in and day out we see incidents involving people who have vanished without a trace, leaving families and authorities scrambling to cobble together the last few days of the missing person's life.[107]

The notion of a Flight Plan steals a bit of jargon from the world of aviation. Flight Plans are merely a statement of when and where the plane intends to go. While it can help with traffic management, the greater importance is that if the plane fails to appear at the other end, we know right away along what path we should start looking. Somebody who is expecting you to arrive may well make the first call when you don't show up as planned.

This habit has the most obvious impact on trips of any length, or when you plan to go somewhere that is outside of your normal area of travel. It can be as simple as a brief word to family or friends, or jotting a note in your own home that would be visible if somebody came looking for you. It can even be in the form of an email you send to yourself or a friend; in the case of a missing person investigators may review your emails to assist their efforts to find you.

---

107   The disappearance of 18-year old Natalee Holloway from a resort in Aruba created a media sensation in the United States. Tragically, like countless other missing persons, Ms. Holloway was never found.

One of the most important times for Flight Planning comes when you go somewhere with a new acquaintance. It is a sad truth that many cases of assault, especially against women, occur as the outcome of some sort of social pretext - a date, a work session, even the simple offer of a ride. In a world where people fill the internet with Instagram photos of things like meals, it is nothing to simply snap a photo of the car you will be riding in, especially where the license plate is visible, and upload it to your hosting site of choice. This may not need to be a covert act; if you pass it off as a hobby (collecting license plates) you may give someone contemplating evil a reason to abandon that pursuit before it begins. Uploading a photo of the people you are with can in similar fashion provide nice memories along with a measure of protection.

Bring a Wingman

There is an old adage that says "there is strength in numbers" and it applies to normal social situations as well. A trusted friend can provide another pair of eyes with which to be aware, and the presence of even one extra person can make the criminal's decision to target you that much more difficult. A good wingman can keep an eye on your behavior and note unexpected changes that might arise from things such as "date rape drugs" which diminish the victim's mental capacity.

There will always be times we want to be alone, and times we our friends are not available. But keep in mind that you are typically better off wherever you go if you have a friend to watch your back. The more isolated or unknown the location, the more you want back-up.

Personal Data Card

Pop quiz: What is your blood type? What is the blood type of your children or your spouse? What about their allergies? These may seem like obscure bits of information but they can be critical in a time of emergency. One of the easiest and yet most valuable things you can do to improve your safety is to collect a set of pertinent information to have on hand when you need it.

A Personal Data Card is a fundamental standard for Executive Protection programs. The idea can easily be adapted for home or community level use. If somebody is hurt or unexpectedly disappears, the information on this form can greatly enhance efforts to rapidly locate and provide possibly critical care.

Many of the fields on this form are self-evident; others may be less so but offer unexpected benefits. Let's take a quick look from top to bottom and highlight some of the less obvious value points.

- **Pictures** can speak a thousand words and a current photo will likely do more than anything else to help authorities or volunteers spot and identify an individual who is missing or injured. This is especially important in the case of missing children or those who are communication-challenged as they may be less responsive to audible outreach efforts.[108] A clear, recent photo can be leveraged in flyers or television coverage. In the case of children, update the photo routinely as kids can change dramatically with age. It may be better to have a "real world" photo rather than a school yearbook picture; a photo used for identification should ideally represent how the person looks on a day-to-day basis.

---

108   Children, elderly and others may be more easily frightened to the point of unresponsiveness. If responders can recognize an individual on sight, rapid identification is more likely.

PHOTO	FIRST NAME	MIDDLE NAME	LAST NAME
	BLOOD TYPE	PASSPORT # & NATION	SSN / NATIONAL ID
	HEIGHT	WEIGHT	MOBILE PHONE NUMBER
	HAIR COLOR	EYE COLOR	MOBILE PHONE IMEI
	OTHER VISIBLE TRAITS: SKIN TONE, BUILD, DISTINGUISHING MARKS, SCARS OR FEATURES		
	LANGUAGES		

ALLERGIES OR ADVERSE REACTION TO:

❏ Penicillin ❏ Sulfa Drugs ❏ Tetracycline ❏ Asperin

❏ Phenytoin ❏ Carbamazepine ❏ Codeine ❏ NSAIDs

❏ Iodine ❏ Other:

MEDICAL HISTORY ITEMS RELEVANT TO URGENT OR CHRONIC CARE

❏ Asthma ❏ Diabetes ❏ Seizures ❏ Anemia

❏ Cancer ❏ Hypertension ❏ Cardiovascular ❏ Deaf / Blind

❏ Other:

NOTES: CURRENT MEDICATIONS ~ NICKNAME ~ SAFE WORD(S)

EMERGENCY CONTACTS	RELATIONSHIP	PHONE	EMAIL

HOME ADDRESS

EMAIL ADDRESS(ES)

VEHICLE MAKE	MODEL	YEAR	LICENSE & STATE	COLOR & UNIQUE FEATURES

SOCIAL MEDIA CONTACT POINTS (SITES & FRIENDS)	

PROOF OF LIFE / DURESS QUESTIONS	CORRECT ANSWER	DURESS ANSWER

- **Nickname** is a point of subtlety that can also have a positive impact dealing with children. Many kids are taught not to talk to strangers and a child who has just been involved in any sort of bad interaction with an adult may be on a far more elevated state of guard, perhaps to the level of panic. If a police officer or responder can use a family nickname it can help forge an immediate connection. Only somebody who had spoken to family would know of such a name and this can be the basis for trust, either to support rescue efforts or merely to ease a child's mind that the Good Guys really are good.

- **Mobile phone number** is obvious, but the **IMEI number** of a mobile phone is not. A 14- to 16-digit number, the IMEI is basically the digital fingerprint of a phone and each one is unique. While Hollywood loves to tell us that police can trace a cell phone call in seconds, the actual process is far more complicated. Technically, things get easier when you have the IMEI number of the phone. This can be used, with co-operation of the service provider, to more quickly correlate a call from that phone to the closest adjacent cell phone tower. In the case of a missing person, reducing the overall area to be searched can greatly enhance the chance of discovery. There are different ways to find the IMEI number, depending on the make and model of phone. If you contact a representative for your phone service or simply Google the make and model of your phone with the term IMEI you can readily find easy instructions.

- **Other Visible Traits** encompass any additional descriptive information about the individual. This may be a description of build, such as lanky or stocky. It may describe tattoos, piercings, scars or blemishes that make this person unique and readily identifiable. The more you can provide with clear specificity, the better. Include anything you think will help an officer to pick your child or missing loved one out of a crowd.

- **Languages** can be important, especially if they do not include the language native to your location. If responders know in advance that a victim speaks only Portuguese or Swahili, they can avoid an extended game of charades and the challenge of playing "what the heck are you saying?" The ability to converse with a victim can be essential in making a swift, safe rescue or conducting urgent medical procedures.

- **Allergies, Medical History and Current Medications** are all important to emergency medical service personnel. Your doctor can help fill in this section if need be. A concise summary will help EMS to confidently provide the best possible care for any injuries or illness a victim is suffering.

- **Social Media** has become a huge part of our lives and most specifically with the younger generations. Kids today can snap photos and upload them to popular sites like Instagram or Imgur in just seconds. These contact points become second-nature and they can be leveraged for news or communication in times of crisis. If you have a list of a subject's social media identities, favored sites or online friends, you may create numerous opportunities to receive information or post data that the subject can readily find.

- **Proof of Life** is a term that arose in the Kidnap and Ransom (K&R) industry. It is a grim notion, basically a question put forward to a kidnapper that can only be answered by the hostage. Much like a password, it is typically a question agreed upon in advance and something that cannot be readily forgotten, like the name of a pet or the title of a favorite book. As Proof of Life questions matured, the notion of a second answer evolved, called a Duress Answer, which would allow a hostage to confirm that the response is being made under some degree of physical threat. For example, if asked to name a favorite superhero, a response of Superman might confirm that a victim is alive and well while Batman confirms he is being held against his will and unable to speak freely. The level of sophistication in Proof of Life / Duress question sets is limitless and members of intelligence and military units have elaborate "code speak" to help convey information to assist in a rescue effort.

- The notion of a **Safe Word** is similar in nature to the Familiar Nickname mentioned above, but with a greater emphasis on positive identification. A Safe Word in this context is a word or phrase that would not likely ever come up in normal conversation or be known "outside of the herd." It is intended to be used by response personnel as a form of quick identification of a hostage or victim. It can be as simple as a single word, like "unicorn" for example, or be a complete phrase such as "The kite is in the tree." The point is that the victim, upon hearing the secret phase, will know that the speaker was entrusted with that information by whatever family or friend who originally created it.

  Groups adopting a Safe Word convention, especially with kids, should periodically make a point of reinforcing the memory and implications of the words. A Safe Word can help establish immediate trust and reduce the chance that fear of the unknown causes a traumatized or confused victim to run away or hide from a would-be rescuer.

A form such as this can be a value in several places. A copy could be put on file at your child's school or at your place of work. (You will need to check with your school to determine its policy on providing information to emergency responders in the event of a crisis.) As an electronic document you can keep a copy on your laptop, tablet or even smartphone, where it could be readily transmitted in a time of need.

Personal Data Kit

Much like a data card, there are documents in your life that you want to have in a crisis, and that is just the time when you may find yourself without your wallet. If your credit card gets stolen, where do you have the card number to report it stolen? Copies of things like your driver's license, passport, medical insurance cards or concealed carry permit may be extremely advantageous in a pinch. An electronic copy may not meet legal criteria in some applications; a digital copy of your passport may not get you out of a foreign country but it could be invaluable in demonstrating reasonable proof of your identity or providing the data needed to verify through other means. If you have a smartphone, the simplest way to assemble such a kit as a digital asset is to take photographs of each document.

CONCLUSION

Many factors prompted the writing of this book. Considerable urging arose from police officers and firefighters who read *The Emergency Responder's Guide to Terrorism* and pointed out a growing need for something similar aimed at non-responders. It was prompted in part by the news that filled my TV screen day in and day out and the awful things that grow more common every day. But in the end it was calls from friends, from family and from neighbors, often in the wake of something breaking in the news, to say they were worried and ask if there was something they could do. I've had friends and colleagues alike ask for an introduction to firearms, some maintaining an aversion to them but wanting to know how they work. Others, sadly, have been touched by violent crime and I see the impact it has had on their lives. I present this book in the hope that it provides some insights, perhaps some new ways to look at your options. It has been reviewed by law enforcement and emergency medical personnel as well as others with experience in high-threat environments around the world, and kindly deemed worthy. I hope you find it as such, and that it provides some bolster to your sense of empowerment, your safety and your peace of mind.